RDR

Black Lenses, Black Voices

GENRE AND BEYOND
A Film Studies Series
Series Editor: Leonard Leff, Oklahoma State University

Genre and Beyond offers fresh perspectives on conceptions of film as well as cinema's role in a changing world. Books in the series explore often overlooked or unconventional genres as well as more traditional themes. These engaging texts have the rigor that scholars demand and the creativity and accessibility that students and interested readers expect.

Titles in the Series

Cinematic Shakespeare
Michael Anderegg

Black Lenses, Black Voices: African American Film Now
Mark A. Reid

Forthcoming in the Series

*High Comedy in American Movies:
Class and Humor from the 1920s to the Present*
Steve Vineberg

Queer Images: Homosexuality in American Film
Harry M. Benshoff and Sean Griffin

Killing in Style: Artistic Murder in the Movies
Steven Schneider

Hybrid Cinema in Hollywood
Ira Jaffe

Film Adaptations
Christine Geraghty

Black Lenses, Black Voices

African American Film Now

Mark A. Reid

ROWMAN & LITTLEFIELD PUBLISHERS, INC.
Lanham • Boulder • New York • Toronto • Oxford

ROWMAN & LITTLEFIELD PUBLISHERS, INC.

Published in the United States of America
by Rowman & Littlefield Publishers, Inc.
A wholly owned subsidiary of The Rowman & Littlefield Publishing Group, Inc.
4501 Forbes Boulevard, Suite 200, Lanham, MD 20706
www.rowmanlittlefield.com

P.O. Box 317, Oxford OX2 9RU, UK

British Library Cataloguing in Publication Information Available

Library of Congress Cataloging-in-Publication Data

Reid, Mark (Mark A.)
  Black lenses, Black voices : African American film now / Mark A. Reid.
    p.   cm.— (Genre and beyond)
  Includes bibliographical references and index.
  ISBN 0-7425-2641-0 (cloth : alk. paper)—ISBN 0-7425-2642-9 (pbk. : alk. paper)   1. African Americans in motion pictures.   2. African Americans in the motion picture industry.   3. Race in motion pictures.   I. Title.   II. Series.
PN1995.9.N4R43   2005
791.43′75′08996073—dc22   2004026201

Printed in the United States of America

⊚ ™ The paper used in this publication meets the minimum requirements of American National Standard for Information Sciences—Permanence of Paper for Printed Library Materials, ANSI/NISO Z39.48-1992.

Contents

In loving memory of my parents,
Robert F. and Patricia M. Reid

Acknowledgments

 $\mathscr{T}$ hanks go to Leonard J. Leff, the series editor, who invited me to write on African American film and was quite helpful in sharpening my prose. I am deeply grateful to Brenda Hadenfeldt, the acquisitions editor, and Jehanne Schweitzer, the production editor, for guiding this book through all its transformations from a very rough draft to an interesting piece of writing.

I would like to thank the dean of the College of Liberal Arts and Sciences at the University of Florida for awarding me a 2002–2003 Humanities Scholarship Enhancement Fund that enabled me to conduct the necessary research to write this book. I would also like to express my gratitude to John Leavey, the English Department chair, who has consistently been supportive of my work in the field of African Diasporic studies.

Most of this book was written and revised in the comfort of a warm Parisian apartment in a neighborhood peopled by North and sub-Saharan Africans, and by Jews and foreign tourists from the States and countries in Western and Eastern Europe. A well-deserved thanks goes to Madame Stora-Burstin for allowing me to write far from the maddening crowd but still in a great multicultural neighborhood that instills a furtive hope for world peace.

This book is an extension of "New Wave Black Cinema in the 1990s," which first appeared in Winston Wheeler Dixon's *Film Genre 2000* (2000). Parts of chapters 1 and 7 of *Redefining Black Film* (1993) were instrumental in shaping the present chapters 1 and 6. This book should be seen as a continuation of *Redefining Black Film*. Chapters 3 and 6, respectively, are expanded versions of earlier essays published in Barry

Grant's *Film Genre Reader II* (1995) and Chris Holmlund and Justin Wyatt's *Contemporary American Independent Film* (2004).

I wish to express my gratitude to a few individuals who have either read the manuscript in its various versions or have read a particular book chapter; all have offered valuable suggestions that, hopefully, render this book more accessible to a general public who may not be familiar with such African Diasporic theoretical approaches as womanism and postNegritude. I am grateful to David Thorstad, to Sylvie Blum, and to Dave Compton, who copyedited this book. A heartfelt thanks goes to Chris Holmlund, who urged me to write more on Haile Gerima's film work.

Finally, I want to express my deep appreciation to the academic and nonacademic organizations that offered me an opportunity to share my research on film and African Diasporic culture. A sincere expression of thanks goes to the Collegium for African American Research, the Modern Language Association, the Society for Cinema and Media Studies, the Texas A&M English Department's General L. M. Lewis Lecture committee, and the French and Swedish American Studies associations.

Introduction

$\mathcal{T}$his book discusses both African American and black-oriented film types, which, when taken together, constitute black film. African American film is any film whose central narrative explores the life and experience of the African Diaspora in the United States. Additionally, the term *African American film* refers only to films directed, written, or cowritten by members of this community. The term *black-oriented film* denotes similar black-focused films whose directors and screenwriters are nonblack.

The construction of the racial subject in popular media and the social and biological sciences continues to be a controversial issue. The way in which scientific and popular media describe blacks resembles the problems encountered when these same institutions attempt sweeping descriptions of Jews, Muslims, Serbs, and Croats. Any attempt to describe these subject identities provokes volatile disagreements between individuals regardless of their race, gender, sexuality, ethnicity, or political hue. Nevertheless, this book offers a tentative description of "black" subjectivity and the term *race* in African American and black-oriented film. This description holds that race is an ever-changing sociocultural construction. Sometimes, national boundaries and local political factors redefine what constitutes the racial and black subject. Rather than biological and genetically assigned characteristics, *race* and *black* are sociological categories. Furthermore, the sociohistorical moment determines the contours of the representation of race. This is what I call a *postNegritude* understanding of race and blackness. The *postNegritude* is a concept that uses a *womanist* theory that is "committed to the survival and wholeness of entire people, male and female. Not a separatist, except periodically, for health. Traditionally universalist. . . . Traditionally capable. . . . Womanist is to feminist as purple to lavender."[1] Previously, scholars have avoided writ-

1

ing about the representation of race in American genre film, although race is very much a part of when and where people of color enter into the camera frame. The same scholars ignore the theoretical importance of womanist approaches to studying gender and sexuality in African American and black-oriented film.

In post–Civil Rights America, the socioeconomic status of African Americans has changed very little as a group, but it may have undergone changes in the case of a select group of exceptional or infamous African American celebrities. There exists a symbiotic relationship between widely distributed black-oriented films and how mainstream news agencies circulate stereotypic images of African Americans. The 2003 news coverage of the alleged sexual crimes of Los Angeles Lakers basketball star Kobe Bryant and music pop star Michael Jackson offer two interesting examples of how visual narratives in both film and news reporting function to entertain and not inform. For instance, the Bryant and Jackson news reports provided graphic descriptions of lurid, sexed-up spectacles—one an alleged rape and the other alleged sex with a minor. This is prime-time material for a cycle of race melodramas of epic proportions. This type of news coverage offers the entertainment industry pulp fictions for broadcast on *Entertainment Tonight* and *Hard Copy* and as televised miniseries or major motion pictures.

Frank Rich, a *New York Times* entertainment critic, admonishes American media and its celebrity-hungry public: "There's not much meat left on Michael Jackson's bones. He is 5 foot 11 and weighs 120 pounds. His face is falling off. But that doesn't mean we can't feast on him for what could be at least a year of what TV calls 'celebrity justice.' "[2] Frank Rich's words evoke a haunting feeling that we are witnessing a racial lynching. How can one avoid the carnal in "there's not much meat left" and not wonder why "his face is falling off"? The moblike cameras and reporters have taken many swipes at Michael Jackson's face, as if camera and reporter were recording while participating in a slasher film or even a racial lynching. Rich criticizes the television coverage. At this historical moment, media conglomerates own television, film, music, and newspaper companies, and film criticism cannot easily separate fictional film from the Michael Jackson news story or its next appearance as a black-oriented film.

Discussions will interrogate the symbiotic relationship between types of film narratives and everyday news reports, because both narratives demonstrate the constructive properties of myths and the dominant narrative forms they rely on. Most often, these everyday narratives determine when and how African Americans enter the camera frame and how they flow from a reporter's newsworthy subjects to a character in a film or novel. This book is about black film and how visual fictional constructions of race and blackness circulate in American film.

Since multinational companies distribute most of the films I examine, it is unwise to believe that any single African American director, regardless of his or her stature in the business, enjoys total artistic control. As a result, these same directors can be complicit in the construction of their community's nefarious screen image; consequently, it is important to consider the various production factors and narrative choices that set many African American and black-oriented mainstream films apart from their nonblack film counterparts. This is equally true for the analysis of the different film styles employed by black directors, writers, and technicians who make black films. Together, these artists and their black film product form a diverse but racially significant social and professional film culture.

This book does not attempt to be encyclopedic; it will offer a selective survey of the various trends in contemporary black filmmaking. The chapters are organized around several popular subgenres, styles, and themes within African American and black-oriented cinema. The first chapter provides a brief history of African American and black-oriented film from their beginnings in 1912 through the late 1940s and ends with a review of the new black renaissance in filmmaking that occurred in the late 1960s through the 1970s. The chapter is a modest, and in no way comprehensive, description of race films made prior to the 1960s and the second wave of black independent filmmaking during the decade following the 1960s.

Using a womanist postNegritude approach, as described above, the subsequent chapters investigate recent African American film—black family, action, horror, and woman-centered films. Chapter 2 covers black family melodrama and focuses on Matty Rich's *Straight Out of Brooklyn* (1991) and *The Inkwell* (1994), George Tillman Jr.'s *Soul Food* (1997), and Kasi Lemmons's *Eve's Bayou* (1997). I have selected these particular films because a black child's reflections drive each film's narrative. The four films depict the lives of northern urban poor, northern middle-class, and Southern rural upper-class black families, respectively. Discussion includes how each film presents the family, its individual family members, and how class, gender, and when pertinent, sexuality construct the representation of the African American family. The narrative issues concerning class, intergenerational, and gender conflicts introduced in this chapter are further developed in the chapters that follow.

Chapter 3 examines recent black directed or written action films. The chapter introduces a brief history of action-oriented black films and directs much of its discussion to the social realist impulse in the selected group of action film. For the purposes of clarification and definition, the black action film includes such action-oriented subgenres as the heist, detective, war, and western subgenres. Chapter 4 covers *Def by Temptation* (1990) and *Bones* (2001), two black-directed, African American horror films. The two films provide a rare opportunity to analyze black horror film and its construction of gender and sexuality as fantastic threats to phallocentric norms and values. The films disrupt everyday notions of gender and sexuality within both hetero- and homosocial spaces.

Chapter 5 turns to African American films that feature female-centered narratives. It studies the hip-hop style and bad girl attitude of Leslie Harris's black independent film *Just Another Girl on the I.R.T.* (1992). The chapter includes F. Gary Gray's female-centered heist film *Set It Off* (1996) and studies the cinematic elements and narrative devices that *Set It Off* shares with male-centered black action films. Adopting a less-than-rigid notion of African American film, chapter 5 also includes Donald Petrie's *The Associate* (1996). The film features Whoopi Goldberg in the leading role, which is quintessentially womanist and postNegritude in her embrace of a nonheterosexist feminism and black consciousness that is not racially exclusive. The final section of this chapter is a selective survey of films in which Halle Berry appears in leading roles. The discussion of Whoopi Goldberg and Halle Berry allows one to investigate black female performance in American sound film.

Chapter 6 extends the study of race and gender in black film to examine Haile Gerima's black independent feature *Sankofa* (1993), including Gerima's alternative production and distribution choices, and gives a close textual analysis of the film narrative. This chapter begins with a short summary of the 1990s news coverage of events that angered, hurt, and embarrassed the African American community. In 1991, television viewers witnessed the videotaped beating of Rodney G. King by several Los Angeles police officers who were subsequently acquitted. During the same year, the Clarence Thomas Senate hearings were widely covered and discussed by news agencies throughout the nation and world. In 1995, viewers were entertained by the O. J. Simpson murder trial. Ironically, three African American males and one black female, Anita Hill, became the talk of the nation. These events brought to national awareness the seamy presence of police brutality, the alleged murder of a white woman by her wealthy and popular black husband, and the sexual harassment of Anita Hill by Clarence Thomas, who would become the second African American appointed to the U.S. Supreme Court. This last offensive item revealed to the world the existence of conservative African Americans who identify with the Republican Party. The black community's reception of Haile Gerima's *Sankofa* was partially an expression of the community's need for an uplifting moral story that visually expressed their particular sociocultural experience. *Sankofa* expressed the blues of enslavement and the necessary violent struggle that African Americans have constantly waged against mental and physical enslavement. The film countered the oppressive images that circulated in broadcast and print news coverage of Simpson, King, and Hill-Thomas. In discussing *Sankofa*, chapter 6 develops the idea of the importance of recalling and witnessing and the necessity of actions that liberate whole people and not merely one individual.

Black participation in Hollywood is as necessary as blacks working in the independent arena. Blacks who work on major studio productions force the lily-white trade and technical unions to integrate blacks into their membership. This is an argument about equal access to Hollywood employment as skilled and well-paid technicians.

The arguments put forth in this book do not express the opinion that if an African American directs or writes a black-oriented film, the filmic representation will be faithful to all African American experiences. Furthermore, the politics of any white or black independent or mainstream filmmaker do not so easily establish a correlation to the film's representational politics, regardless of whether it is progressive, centrist, conservative, or fascist. This is also true for any visual representation of the black female in a leading and supporting role; and this is why chapter 5 analyzes the white-directed and white-written film *The Associate*, distributed by Buena Vista Pictures. The film is a rare example of a black female–centered film that features the black woman practicing, rather than contemplating, womanist ideas. As cultural critic Stuart Hall has said, there are no guarantees. The film highlights the unfixed nature of films made and distributed by such multinational conglomerates as Disney.

Black Lenses, Black Voices is about the actors, writers, filmmakers, technicians, businesspersons, and audiences who, through their participation as both producers and consumers, give life to this particular art form. Film audiences, no matter how meek they might be, do produce their own narratives when watching films. This book is but an example of such a narrative production in response to watching and reflecting on how American media constructs African Americans in several contemporary films. Further examinations in this area of film and visual culture would be wise to study black independent cinema to show how issues concerning distribution, production, and casting affect the visual aesthetics and politics of groups of black films, the industry, and the audiences who frequent such films.

NOTES

1. Alice Walker, *In Search of Our Mothers' Gardens: Womanist Prose by Alice Walker* (New York: Harcourt Brace Jovanovich, 1983), xi. Also see Sherley Anne Williams, "Some Implications of Womanist Theory," in *Reading Black, Reading Feminist*, ed. Henry Louis Gates Jr., 68–75 (New York: Meridian, 1990).

2. Frank Rich, "America Tunes in for the Money Shot," *New York Times*, 30 November 2003, 1, 28. "Mr. Jackson's sole entertainment value for some time . . . has been as a freak. To say that we care about him now because he's a celebrity or a pop star or an alleged criminal is to sanitize both his real appeal and the audience's sleazy complicity in his spectacle. People are turned on by the Jackson story because it's about sex" (1).

• 1 •

Early African American Film, 1912–1940 and Beyond

EARLY AFRICAN AMERICAN FILMS WERE
NOT CALLED "BLAXPLOITATION"

ℬlack-directed action films depicting urban life in Los Angeles, New York, Chicago, and elsewhere predate the mid-1970s appearance of black action films. Before and immediately after World War I, black filmmakers produced short comedies, family melodramas, and black action films.

From 1912 to 1918, blacks directed short documentaries, comedies, family melodramas, and action films. They featured African Americans as soldiers, businessmen, political leaders, celebrities, and adventurers seeking their fortunes in the West. The Foster Photoplay Company was the first African American independent film company. According to film historian Thomas R. Cripps, William Foster probably was the earliest black to direct a film. Cripps describes Foster: "A clever hustler from Chicago, he had been a press agent for the [Bert] Williams and [George] Walker revues and [Bob] Cole and Johnson's *A Trip to Coontown* [circa 1898], a sportswriter for the [Chicago] *Defender*, an occasional actor under the name of Juli Jones, and finally a purveyor of sheet music and Haitian coffee. He may have made the first black movie, *The Railroad Porter*, an imitation of Keystone comic chases completed perhaps three years before *The Birth of a Nation* [8 February 1915]."[1] The Johnson brothers— George Perry (a U.S. postal employee) and Noble (a Universal Pictures contract actor)—established the Lincoln Motion Picture Company in 1916. The Lincoln Motion Picture Company excelled in racial uplift and

7

black soldiering movies. The company produced four middle-class melo-dramas—*The Realization of a Negro's Ambition* (1916), *The Trooper of Troop K* (1916), *A Man's Duty* (1920), and *By Right of Birth* (1921)—and ended producing films with a one-reel documentary, *A Day with the Famous 10TH* (1921), about the black Tenth Cavalry stationed at Fort Huachuca, Arizona. Lincoln Motion Picture Company always featured a black vir-tuous hero who is driven by the Protestant work ethic. Lincoln films avoided lengthy dramatizations of criminality or drunk, vulgar, and licen-tious behavior, and their films promoted racially uplifting narratives in which the black hero reaps material and spiritual rewards for adhering to the Protestant work ethic.

In 1919, Oscar Micheaux wrote, directed, and produced his first film, *The Homesteader*. He made twenty-five more silent films during the nearly ten years before his film company went bankrupt in 1928. As Ger-ald R. Butters Jr. notes, "Monetary gain from filmmaking was always a priority for Micheaux. In February 1928, at the end of the silent era, he was forced to file for bankruptcy. He reorganized in 1929 under the title The Micheaux Film Corporation with an infusion of white capital."[2] Micheaux made films that explored such controversial issues as racial lynching, interracial intimacy, racial passing, urban poverty, and crimi-nality.[3]

From their very independent beginnings to the present, African American filmmakers have treated similar black-oriented themes and social issues within popular genre forms. These filmmakers injected black cultural content into the western, musical, family melodrama, detective, and gangster film genres. Admittedly, early black filmmakers used a cine-matic style that was limited by the technology of the day and the film-maker's modest production budget.

In the 1930s through the 1940s, white producers and theater man-agers such as Alfred Sack of Sack Amusement and Leo Brecher and Frank Schiffman, managers of Harlem's Apollo Theater, financed Oscar Micheaux's films and other black-directed or black-written films.[4] Since these small companies and individuals were independent of the major Hollywood studios—Fox Film Corporation, Metro-Goldwyn-Mayer, Warner Brothers, and the like—the race films produced and distributed by the smaller businesses are vastly different from such Hollywood stu-dio–financed black-oriented musical films as *Hearts in Dixie* (Fox, 1929), *Hallelujah!* (MGM, 1929), *The Green Pastures* (Warner, 1936), and *Cabin in the Sky* (MGM, 1942). To this day, major studios attract some of the most talented black stage and screen actors, employ highly skilled technicians, and use the most up-to-date film technology, which independent filmmakers and productions cannot afford unless they have some business affiliation with the majors, as does Spike Lee. Neither the black independent filmmaker nor the white-controlled small companies that produced black-oriented films could afford such an expensive production overhead. Thus, these white angels provided black filmmakers with a means to continue directing black-oriented film fare and enter the sound film era. This interracial business relationship, which lasted from 1930 through 1948, permitted Oscar Micheaux to make his first sound film, *The Exile* (1931).[5] Micheaux made sixteen more sound films during this eighteen-year period without support from Hollywood studios. Black-directed and black-oriented films produced between 1912 and the 1940s, commonly referred to as "race films," exhibit distinct differences in technical skill compared to the post-1970s black films made by university-trained filmmakers and black directors whose projects were funded or distributed by major studios. In most, if not all, instances, whether black filmmakers worked for large companies or worked independently, they wanted their films to entertain and educate their audiences and make a sufficient profit to finance their next film.

The second renaissance in black independent filmmaking occurred during the late 1960s and 1970s and saw the development of the independently produced social documentary and the fiction film. African American documentary film and video were made for the program needs of television news magazines covering such domestic issues as black urban America, the Civil Rights and Black Power movements, and the anti-imperialist struggles in Africa, the Caribbean, and other parts of the world. During this period, black filmmakers and videographers were employed by television news programs and government agencies or were contracted by not-for-profit agencies to produce a single work. Black documentary filmmakers such as Madeline Anderson, Carroll Parrott Blue, St. Clair Bourne, Kathleen Collins, Charles Hobson, and Stan Lathan worked for television news programs.[6] William Greaves, the most prolific black documentary artist, worked for governmental agencies, not-for-profit agencies, and news magazine programs.[7]

Black independent fiction filmmakers supplied the growing number of independent movie theaters, international film festivals, and educational venues that welcomed black independent cinema and black-oriented films. The first of this group was the novelist-filmmaker-playwright Melvin Van Peebles, who began filmmaking as an independent filmmaker and whose first works were short documentaries, before he garnered international fame at the 1968 San Francisco Film Festival with the feature-length film *The Story of a Three-Day Pass* (1968). As early as 1970, Van Peebles directed and wrote *Watermelon Man* for Columbia Pictures, which was followed by the independently produced *Sweet Sweetback's Baadasssss Song* (Cinemation, 1971).

Very different from Melvin Van Peebles, who was not university trained and alternated between work inside and outside of Hollywood, and unlike the 1960s documentary artists, the late 1960s to mid-1970s university-trained black filmmakers Charles Burnett, Julie Dash, Haile Gerima, Warrington Hudlin, and Alile Sharon Larkin chose to work outside Hollywood. In the 1990s, however, Burnett and Dash made several films for major studios and for broadcast on television.[8]

A NEW WAVE OF BLACK INDEPENDENT
FEATURE FILMMAKERS: PARADIGM SHIFT

During the late 1970s, many black independent filmmakers received technical training in white educational institutions. As might be expected, Los Angeles seemed to attract the largest group of black filmmakers. The philosophy of black consciousness and the writings and speeches of African leaders such as Ghana's Kwame Nkrumah, Guinea's Sékou Touré, and Congo's Patrice Lumumba influenced many of these black students. Such filmmakers as Charles Burnett, Larry Clark, Julie Dash, Haile Gerima, Alile Sharon Larkin, and Billy Woodberry, all graduates from Los Angeles films schools or institutes, rejuvenated the then-languishing black independent film movement.

This new generation of West Coast filmmakers, and East Coast contemporaries such as St. Clair Bourne, rejected the imposed conditions of mainstream American cinema because it limited their artistic and political vision of black life and experience. In their rejection of Hollywood, these filmmakers not only rejuvenated black independent film but also created a paradigm shift in the history of black independent filmmaking. Haile Gerima describes at what point he became aware of this shift:

> I left UCLA before I even got my degree. I graduated, didn't go to the celebration or anything, went across the country to come

teach at Howard in Washington D.C. Even then, I couldn't imagine how a white supremacist structure such as Hollywood, an industry of culture that has created havoc to all human beings, could be a base for me to peacefully tell my story and experiment. Hollywood didn't have any obligation to tolerate my search in form. The only term that Hollywood accepts is the commercial mold. And once you cease to operate within that paradigm, the industry will reject all the reasons you have to tell a story. So that was clear to me when I was a student at UCLA.[9]

Similar to the first wave of black independent filmmakers such as Oscar Micheaux, the new generation worked in the shadows of mainstream film. Unlike Micheaux and other black independent filmmakers between the two world wars, Gerima and many members of this new generation used abstract and experimental film styles and articulated a politics of black nationalism. This separated them from their American contemporaries, black and nonblack, who attended the same film schools but opted to speak to mainstream audiences and acquire major studio financing and distribution. This new generation of black filmmakers chose to work outside the production gates of the neighboring studios. They borrowed the politics, film styles, and narrative forms that were being used by African, Latin American, Asian, and European filmmakers who also worked outside of Hollywood conventions and norms.

A few critics have referred to this West Coast phenomenon as an "L.A. rebellion." One can also view this as a shifting paradigm in which American filmmakers recognized that Hollywood was not the only cinema and, instead, sought to participate in an international film movement that included such filmmakers as Jean-Luc Godard, Alain Resnais, Sarah Maldoror, Gillo Pontecorvo, and Ousmane Sembene. Thus, the so-called L.A. rebellion was not as local as it may have seemed at the time. This generation of black filmmakers was influenced by international trends in cinema as well as their international student colleagues and teachers. Theirs was an organic rebellion of international proportions that reflected what was going on in Vietnam, the People's Republic of China, and Africa. It was not simply about a racial angst, but race concerns were very much a part of the mix, along with considerations of class and gender inequities.[10]

The first wave of university-trained black filmmakers (Haile Gerima, Charles Burnett, Larry Clark, Billy Woodberry, Julie Dash, and Alile

Sharon Larkin) rejuvenated the black independent feature-film movement, which had been languishing since the decade following World
War II. All six of these student filmmakers earned their master of fine arts
degrees in film production at either the University of California at Los
Angeles or the University of Southern California, or in the case of Dash,
"studied film production at the City College of New York and studied
directing at the American Film Institute and the University of California,
both in Los Angeles."[11] After a quarter century, Haile Gerima and Larry
Clark never abandoned their independent beginnings. I discuss Gerima's
work in the last chapter of this book.

This new group of blacks used different film styles that were influenced by European and postcolonial film movements, but their films
were focused on the African American community, as the earliest black
filmmakers had done before them. Italian neorealism and the French
New Wave cinematic styles inform certain black independent films of
this period.[12] The distinguishing characteristics of black independent film
are the handheld camera's trembling movement, the urban location for
shooting, discontinuous editing, and bad lighting. This reflects a lack of
money, which is, interestingly, the same factor that determined the look
of Italian neorealism and French New Wave film styles. In the area of
film content, the films made by the university-trained blacks are influenced by the works of their African, Latin American, Caribbean, and
Asian contemporaries, whose films shared an interest in exploring urban
poverty, police brutality, and the life experiences of black and other third
world women, as portrayed in the films of Gerima, Dash, and Larkin.[13]

This post-1960s renaissance also included a more mainstream group
of black filmmakers whose films were produced and distributed by major
Hollywood studios; these films included Gordon Parks's *The Learning
Tree* (Warner, 1969) and *Shaft* (MGM, 1971), Gordon Parks Jr.'s *Superfly*
(Warner, 1972), and Ossie Davis's *Black Girl* (Cinerama, 1972). Although
there are exceptions, most black Hollywood filmmakers during the 1970s
did not attend university film schools. One explanation for this is that the
phenomenon of university-trained filmmakers was new and was especially novel for African Americans. Still, both university-trained and
black Hollywood filmmakers employed African American actors, used
popular black music forms, and borrowed from existing American film
genres. Unlike their independent counterparts, black Hollywood films,
especially those in the African American action-film genre, exploit the

more exotic elements of the black American experience, as was the case for Oscar Micheaux's sound films.

AFRICAN AMERICAN FILM NOW

During the 1990s, blacks directed many films, but many of these directors began their careers as actors, writers, editors, cinematographers, assistant directors, or film producers. For instance, Vondie Curtis-Hall, Bill Duke, Spike Lee, Kasi Lemmons, Mario Van Peebles, and Forest Whitaker are well-known directors who have had important acting careers. Moreover, the actor-directors Curtis-Hall, Lee, Lemmons, and Van Peebles wrote the scripts for their respective films *Gridlock'd* (Polygram, 1997), *He Got Game* (Touchstone, 1998), *Eve's Bayou* (Trimark, 1997), and *Posse* (Polygram, 1993). Another significant number of African American directors started as cinematographers, producers, or director-writers for black-directed films. Ernest Dickerson, the director–writer of *Juice* (Paramount, 1992), was Lee's preferred cinematographer during the 1980s. Douglas McHenry produced such black action films as *New Jack City* (Warner, 1991) and *The Walking Dead* (Savoy Pictures, 1995). McHenry also codirected *House Party II* (Avco-Embassy, 1991) and directed *Jason's Lyric* (Polygram, 1994). Darnell Martin, one of the few black women directors in Hollywood, was second assistant camera on Lee's *Do the Right Thing* (Universal Pictures, 1989). She went on to write and direct *I Like It Like That* (Columbia Pictures, 1994).

The widening opportunities and interchangeable roles for African Americans as director-writers, director-producers, or cinematographers of major films show that Hollywood has become an important outlet for a significant group of black film artists and technicians. But its liberal capitalistic openness to employing talented blacks might have its drawbacks. For instance, would-be black independent filmmakers, writers, and technicians are attracted to Hollywood's equal opportunity employment practices, which lessen the availability of skilled black technicians for independent black film productions. During the earliest period of American film, black independent filmmaking lost talented actors to a Hollywood that was willing to hire them. From the 1920s through the 1940s, major American studios attracted the most talented black stage actors who sought fame and a weekly paycheck, which was not available from the black independent film companies. Since the late 1960s, major motion picture companies have attracted African Americans to direct and perform in black-oriented films as well as nonblack film fare. Again, this selective openness to hire blacks as performers, technicians, writers, and directors precludes the studio's executive board. In sum, this racial ceiling in the American film industry hurts the growth of black independent cinema and limits African American participation in the corporate structure of the American film industry.

The lure of Hollywood took Spike Lee from his independent film beginnings but has done little to damage Lee's artistry. In fact, Lee has probably benefited from his more than a decade of filmmaking in Hollywood. However, Columbia Pictures botched the marketing and distribution of Charles Burnett's *To Sleep with Anger* (1990), a film that was black directed, written, and produced. Columbia's minuscule distribution of Burnett's *To Sleep* is but one example of how a studio can stifle a film that features a talented African American cast in a challenging black family film. Yet there are indeed black-directed and black-written Hollywood films that present similar sociocultural themes and use innovative visual styles, such as the 1970s black independent films by Charles Burnett, Larry Clark, Julie Dash, Haile Gerima, and Alile Sharon Larkin.

Political concerns, black urban music, and visual styles simmer in the 1990s black Hollywood films directed and written by such artists as Bill Duke, Spike Lee, Kasi Lemmons, Darnell Martin, John Singleton, and George Tillman Jr. These filmmakers demonstrate that resourceful and committed filmmakers can find honest work in an industry that produces for an international market. Their films are critical to the growth of black Hollywood and the American film industry. I do not mean that audiences should applaud every black-directed and black-written film. One must distinguish which films are well made and why. Filmmaking requires several talented individuals—director, writer, editor, cinematographer, producer, and others. One should not confuse or overestimate the decision-making power any member of the film crew may have over the final film product. One must always study several different sources. Still, studied criticism cannot escape the fact that it is far from being an objective act. Film criticism employs subjective criteria that some film critics agree with and others disagree with. The African American audience's critical reception of *The Color Purple* (both Alice Walker's 1982 novel and Steven Spielberg's 1985 film) illustrates how diverse this reception can be within any community that is defined by identity politics.[14]

Yet the last two decades of black Hollywood films create Molotov cocktails containing black populist politics, rap music, and innovative camera techniques. After their visual and auditory explosions, filmgoers are left with images of mob rule and the results of black-on-black butchery. This abuse of opportunity by certain black filmmakers furnishes them with a fast buck and premature *jouissance*, just as happens in their films. The black-directed and black-written films that celebrate nihilism and senseless killing are far different from black Hollywood films made by Lee, Lemmons, Singleton, and black independent filmmakers who work with less financial support and fewer distribution outlets.

More to the point, if black filmmakers only made art house films, major studios would not finance and distribute their works—or would they? "No" would be too easy a response. There are a few exceptions to this rule of thumb that require comment. Indeed, studios have financed and distributed several black-directed art house films that treat controversial issues and use an experimental or avant-garde film style. Kasi Lemmons's *Eve's Bayou* (1997) and *The Caveman's Valentine* (2001) are two recent examples of this. Here, "Hollywood marketability" refers to and results from working for a major film organization—though merely directing and writing major studio-produced films does not guarantee any filmmaker this distinction. The film must attract a box office that equals three or more times the production and marketing costs of the film, or it must attract critical acclaim.

A case in point is Forest Whitaker's screen adaptation of Terry McMillan's 1992 best-selling novel *Waiting to Exhale*. Whitaker's 1995 film, produced and distributed by Twentieth Century Fox, grossed more than $66 million in domestic rentals (the box-office receipts). The film's production and marketing costs amounted to about $15 million. The box-office success of *Waiting to Exhale* provides Whitaker and McMillan with Hollywood marketability. Consequently, Whitaker acquired more options for his next Twentieth Century Fox project, *Hope Floats* (1998), received a production budget of $30 million, and signed Sandra Bullock as featured actress. Thus, he received a larger production budget and better choices over the talent and crew for his next project. This explains why a box-office success offers any director better opportunities to receive a larger production budget for the next film project. Still, it does not explain why Spike Lee, after many box-office failures, retains a discernible amount of professional prestige in Hollywood. Lee has consistently made moderately important sociopolitical films for more than two decades, and has done this within Hollywood. His most flawed films continue to attract varying opinions on their critical merit. And Lee's critical and box-office successes—*She's Gotta Have It* (Island Pictures, 1986), *Do the Right Thing* (Universal Pictures, 1989), and *He Got Game* (Touchstone, 1998)—keep him afloat after his numerous *Titanics* have sunk. Finally, Lee's victorious struggle to produce and distribute *Malcolm X* (Warner Brothers, 1992) and *Get On the Bus* (Columbia Pictures, 1996) is unequaled among his Hollywood contemporaries.

NOTES

1. Thomas R. Cripps, *Slow Fade to Black* (New York: Oxford University Press, 1977), 79–80.

2. Gerald R. Butters Jr., *Black Manhood on the Silent Screen* (Lawrence: University Press of Kansas, 2002), 149.

3. For information on the work of Oscar Micheaux, see Mark A. Reid, *Redefining Black Film* (Berkeley: University of California Press, 1993); J. Ronald Green, *Straight Lick: The Cinema of Oscar Micheaux* (Bloomington: Indiana University Press, 2000); and Pearl Bowser, Jane Gaines, and Charles Musser, eds., *Oscar Micheaux and His Circle: African-American Filmmaking and Race Cinema of the Silent Era* (Bloomington: Indiana University Press, 2001).

4. Cripps, *Slow Fade to Black*, 251.

5. Cripps, *Slow Fade to Black*, 323.

6. Kathleen Collins received her B.A. in philosophy and religion from Skidmore College and, as a graduate student, did work in French literature and film, for which she earned an M.A. and a Ph.D. from Middlebury Graduate School of French. See Phyllis R. Klotman, *Screenplays of the African American Experience* (Bloomington: Indiana University Press, 1991), 123.

7. For a focused discussion on William Greaves, see Reid, *Redefining Black Film*. For a comprehensive list of blacks working in documentary film, see Phyllis R. Klotman and Janet K. Cutler, eds., *Struggles for Representation: African American Documentary Film and Video* (Bloomington: Indiana University Press, 1999).

8. Charles Burnett's nonindependent work includes TV's *America Becoming* (1991) and the major studio works *To Sleep with Anger* (Samuel Goldwyn, 1990) and *The Glass Shield* (Miramax, 1995). Julie Dash's nonindependent work has been for television broadcast and includes *Subway Stories* (1996), *Funny Valentines* (1998), *Incognito* (1998), *Love Song* (2001), and *The Rosa Parks Story* (2002).

9. Haile Gerima, "Interview with Haile Gerima," by Anne Crémieux, Washington, D.C., March 2001, at www.africultures.com/actualite/sorties/anglais/gerima.htm.

10. Haile Gerima chastises black film criticism in a most scornful tone, disassociating himself from the black film critic–scholar: "They took us as perfect filmmakers at that early age, when we were still awkward filmmakers. So there is no dialectical relationship. We gave them birth, but they don't even challenge us as filmmakers. They only want to coexist incestuously. It is a side effect of a general systemic problem. . . . [T]hey were students at the university. . . . [T]hey didn't know what to do with us and they just fantasized us and admired us falsely because they were as hungry as us. We came shooting in all directions. It was chaotic. They said we were masters, 'the LA rebellion,' the LA bullshit, names left and right, the filmmakers were the only people who said 'wait a minute.' . . . Then the critics came. It became a turf. It became a section territory for tenure and Ph.D. degree getting. And the art, the struggle, the revolution was abandoned. So we are now in our own placenta. We cannot be born again." Gerima, "Interview with Haile Gerima."

11. Melvin Donalson, *Black Directors in Hollywood* (Austin: University of Texas Press, 2003), 179. See also Klotman, *Screenplays of the African American Experience*, 191. Describing Julie Dash's film education, Klotman writes: "After earning her B.A. degree in film production [at City College of New York], Dash moved to Los Angeles and attended the Center for Advanced Film Studies at the American Film Institute. . . . [S]he conceived and directed an experimental dance film, *Four Women* (1977). . . . That same year, as a graduate film student at UCLA, she directed *Diary for an African Nun* . . . [and] it earned her a Director's Guild Award for student film." Thus, Dash can easily be considered part of the West Coast black independent film movement of the late 1970s.

12. For a filmic illustration of Italian neorealism, see Warrington Hudlin's social documentary *Street Corner Stories* (1977) and Charles Burnett's family melodrama *Killer of Sheep* (1977).

13. African American independent fiction films that exemplify this attention to black female subjectivity include, but are not limited to, Haile Gerima's *Bush Mama* (1976); Julie Dash's *Four Women* (1977), *Diary of an African Nun* (1978), and *Illusions* (1983); and Alile Sharon Larkin's *A Different Image* (1981).

14. Important issues concerning feminist and black womanist film reception are discussed in Barbara Smith, "Towards a Black Feminist Criticism," in *The New Feminist Criticism*, ed. Elaine Showalter, 4–18 (New York: Pantheon, 1985); Mel Watkins, "Sexism, Racism and Black Women Writers," *New York Times Book Review*, 12 June 1986, 1, 35–37; Diane Carson, Linda Dittmar, and Janice Welsch, eds., *Multiple Voices in Feminist Film Criticism* (Minneapolis: University of Minnesota Press, 1994); and Jacqueline Bobo, *Black Women as Cultural Readers* (New York: Columbia University Press, 1995). There is an equally important discussion of how African American audiences constitute many types of receptions in Trudier Harris, "On *The Color Purple*, Stereotypes, and Silence," *Black American Literature Forum* 18 (1984): 155–61.

· 2 ·

Black Family Film: The 1990s

$\mathcal{W}$e can explore the filmic portrayals of different socioeconomic classes of the contemporary African American family in African American directed and written black family melodramas such as Matty Rich's *Straight Out of Brooklyn* (Samuel Goldwyn, 1991) and *The Inkwell* (Buena Vista Pictures, 1994), George Tillman Jr.'s *Soul Food* (Twentieth Century Fox, 1997), and Kasi Lemmons's *Eve's Bayou* (Trimark, 1997). Each film also dramatizes contemporary social issues that challenge the family's moral integrity and group stability. *Straight Out of Brooklyn* provides a despondent image of the father–son relationship that indicates that the son may follow the same downward spiral as his father. Matty Rich's second feature, *The Inkwell*, relates a difficult father–son relationship that ends with the son's passage into manhood and the reconciliation of all three family members, father, mother, and son.

WORKING URBAN POOR AND
MIDDLE-CLASS FAMILY FILM

Matty Rich's *Straight Out of Brooklyn* is set in a predominantly black New York City neighborhood. Visually, the film negotiates black-and-white cinematography, handheld camera movement, claustrophobic interiors, and distraught black parents in very much the same manner as Burnett's *Killer of Sheep* (1977), which is set in an equally impoverished black Los Angeles community. *Straight Out* presents a mass of tall public housing complexes that tower over their black inhabitants. Sounds are not of silence, but of police sirens mixed with gunfire that echo off the housing development's cold, hard cement walls. The exterior daylight scenes infer the degree to which lower-class urban blacks have been contained in prison-like settings that police inspect as blacks receive and deliver indiscriminate violence. Rich's interior scenes are claustrophobic, even though the rooms are scantily decorated. The sound of a loud drunken man abusing his wife replaces the police sirens and anonymous gunfire that await anyone attempting to escape this interior for the mean streets. Burnett's *Killer* invokes a similar picture of the souring of black families who suffer from unemployment and underemployment.

Burnett uses scenes of sheep at slaughter and empty exterior spaces that exist uncomfortably between dilapidated single-family housing. Burnett's interior scenes reveal the inner lives of the souls of black folk whom he films. Theirs are the emptied private moments in which the black couple has nothing to say to each other. A single tear wells up in the eye of the mother, the father is speechless and full of hurt, their pre-adolescent daughter witnesses not spousal abuse, but something that is just as bad. The couple's long silence is as heartbreaking as Rich's scene of the loud fight between the couple in *Straight Out*. Are these two filmmakers predicting that the youths who witness their parents' lives will soon become them? The two filmmakers stress how certain black families are destroyed by economic conditions. They avoid showy spectacles that celebrate images of imprudent young blacks who turn to crime to seek wealth, fast cars, and fine clothes.

Borrowing the gritty color cinematography of Melvin Van Peebles's *Sweet Sweetback's Baadasssss Song* (1971), Haile Gerima's *Bush Mama* (1975), and Larry Clark's *Passing Through* (1977), Ernest Dickerson's *Juice* (1992) presents exterior scenes filled with concrete-and-brick buildings that stand in close proximity to asphalt streets. There is no hint of greenery or park settings. Unlike the menacing presence of police officers in *Sweetback* and unsympathetic welfare workers in *Bush Mama*, *Juice* presents juveniles who dominate every frame with fistfights and knife play that establish their violent sense of manhood. In hindsight, the violence dramatized in *Juice* is less spectacular than that shown in such adolescent male films as *Boyz N the Hood* and *Menace II Society*. In fact, adolescent males establish their masculinity through gun battles with rival gangs. Guns are not freely distributed nor are they respected by most of the characters in this film. However, a gun leads to the death of at least two black males. This particular action-oriented black family-film subgenre borrows its naturalistic elements from such African American literary works as Richard Wright's *Native Son* (1940), which explores urban pov-

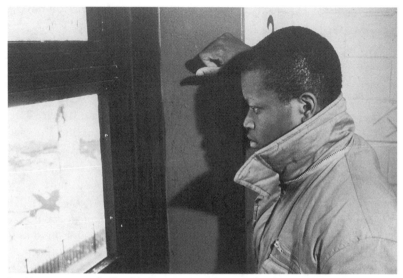

Looking at a mass of tall public housing complexes with a furtive thought to his future or the lack of one: Larry Gilliard Jr. as Dennis Brown in Matty Rich's *Straight Out of Brooklyn* (1991). (Samuel Goldwyn Productions / The Kobal Collection)

erty, black masculinity, adolescent criminality, and the American justice system. Many of these elements are also in the black action film, which is discussed in chapter 3. Another subgenre of the black family film is the middle-class melodrama. The films in this subgenre are less concerned with the destructive elements of urban poverty, criminality, and social injustice. Their narratives are more concerned with class mobility, family unity, and celebrations of blacks who successfully endure racism and poverty. Still, this subgenre occasionally presents black family members who will never acquire the American Dream.

The black middle-class family film presents family members in struggles with growing divisions within the black extended-family unit. Family discord develops when the financially successful member unwittingly humiliates the less educated or financially successful member. This class conflict narrative appears in such middle-class family melodramas as Charles Burnett's *To Sleep with Anger* (Columbia Pictures, 1990); Spike Lee's *Jungle Fever* (Universal Pictures, 1991), *Crooklyn* (Universal Pictures, 1994), and *He Got Game* (Touchstone, 1998); Matty Rich's *The Inkwell* (Buena Vista Pictures, 1994); and George Tillman Jr.'s *Soul Food*

(Twentieth Century Fox, 1997). I turn now to a discussion of how this conflict is present in *The Inkwell*.

The Inkwell presents two sisters and their families spending a summer together at the "Inkwell," the middle- to upper-middle-class black section of Martha's Vineyard, Massachusetts. Here, African Americans who can afford such luxuries escape to their large seaside vacation homes along the Atlantic Ocean. A sixteen-year-old Drew Tate (Larenz Tate) and his parents Kenny (Joe Morton) and Brenda (Suzzanne Douglas) form a working-class nuclear family. The composition of the black family represents an imagined normative family, regardless of race and class. Kenny is a social worker and former member of the Black Panther Party. He remains committed to socially progressive ideas and endeavors. His past and present political idealism, rather than apathy, make Kenny far from the American norm. Kenny reluctantly drives from Wilmington, North Carolina, to the vacation home of his in-laws. Brenda, however, is thrilled that she will see her upper-middle-class sister Francis Phillips (Vanessa Bell Calloway), her black Republican brother-in-law Spencer (Glynn Turman), their son Junior (Duane Martin), and her stern but

The meeting of sisters, a mother, and her grandson spark class conflicts: Suzzanne Douglass as Brenda Tate, Vanessa Bell Calloway as Francis Phillips, Larenz Tate as Drew Tate, and Mary Alice as Evelyn in Matty Rich's *The Inkwell* (1994). (Giant Pictures / The Kobal Collection)

loveable, upper-middle-class mother Evelyn (Mary Alice). The film comically explores the initial contempt that Kenny's brother-in-law and mother-in-law, Spencer and Evelyn, have for his leftist politics and low-paying job. When speaking to her daughter Brenda about Kenny, Evelyn uses the scornful tag "the Black Panther." She mockingly asks Brenda, "How is the Black Panther doing?" The "Black Panther" reference indicates Kenny's historical past and the source for his present community-based sociopolitical values. When Evelyn utters "the Black Panther," it expresses her prejudicial feelings toward black leftists as primitive and condemned to repeat past mistakes rather than reaping the benefits of affirmative action in the capitalist marketplace that has afforded Inkwell blacks, such as her son-in-law Spencer, vacation homes on Martha's Vineyard.

It was the summer of 1976. A photograph of Richard Nixon and one of Booker T. Washington adorn one of the walls of the Tate's Martha's Vineyard summer home. Francis does not participate in Spencer's inane badgering of Kenny. Brenda remains at a safe distance. Still, in certain scenes the sisters perform the sibling rivalry of their adolescent past to a comical degree similar to the political brouhaha between their husbands. In one hilarious scene, Spencer challenges Kenny to a tennis match and wagers a bet based on his assumption that Kenny has never played a serious game of tennis since he disapproves of bourgeois leisure life. Kenny halfheartedly accepts the challenge. To Spencer's surprise, Kenny wins all the sets and shames Spencer for the loss. Consequently, Spencer, to regain his self-esteem and maintain class pretensions, proceeds to physically challenge Kenny. Again, Kenny proves to be morally and physically Spencer's superior. Kenny deflects several of Spencer's awkward martial arts attacks before he gives Spencer his comeuppance. Consistent with the film's playful attitude toward their political differences, both men nurse minor bruises from their fisticuffs and end the film with mutual respect for the other's political opinions.

As political battle wounds heal for Kenny and Spencer, so do marital wounds, as Kenny and Brenda return to the harmony and love they enjoyed in the distant past. Drew also has a spiritual wound and carries guilt for having accidentally started a fire that almost destroyed his parents' house. Ironically, the trip to Martha's Vineyard leads to the antidote for all the wounds—political sectarianism, familial love lost, and Drew's shame. Drew's deflowering by an older woman liberates him from his previous social inadequacies (he carries around a doll that he converses with rather than developing friendships with his adolescent male and female peers).

For Drew, the summer stay at Martha's Vineyard permits him to emotionally mature and become the young man that his father desires him to be. He rooms with his womanizing cousin Junior. The two form a classic comical pair. The skirt-chasing Junior is to passive and virginal Drew as suave Dean Martin was to awkward Jerry Lewis. Junior clumsily delivers overused pick-up lines to persuade the vacationing African American teenage girls to spend time with him and his two equally bumbling fools of best friends, Darryl (Markus Redmond) and Moe (Perry Moore).

From afar, Drew sees Lauren Kelly (Jada Pinkett Smith) on the beach at sunset and becomes enraptured. Later, he sees her reclined on the beach and cautiously approaches with an obscure poem, and she dismisses him. His interest in Lauren increases, and so does his determination. Lauren offers Drew a second opportunity when she sees her boyfriend with another girl and agrees to see him to make her boyfriend

Brothers-in-law of different class and political affiliations take it to the tennis courts: Joe Morton as Kenny Tate, Suzzanne Douglas as Brenda Tate, Glynn Turman as Spencer Phillips, and Vanessa Bell Calloway as Francis Phillips in Matty Rich's *The Inkwell* (1994). (Giant Pictures / The Kobal Collection)

A summer romance turns into a drama of self-awareness for one virginal lad: Larenz Tate as Drew Tate and Jada Pinkett Smith as Lauren Kelly in Matty Rich's *The Inkwell* (1994). (Giant Pictures / The Kobal Collection)

jealous. Concurrently, Drew meets Heather Lee (A. J. Johnson), a married woman in her late twenties for whom he helps carry groceries. After discovering the adulterous nature of her husband Harold (Morris Chestnut), Drew creates harmless disasters to scare him into monogamy. His chivalrous attempts are unsuccessful, but they provoke Heather's admiration.

Like Heather, who discovers that her husband is an unrepentant adulterer, Drew discovers that Lauren merely has used him to reawaken her boyfriend's desire. The day that Lauren has promised to spend with Drew she spends with her boyfriend, making love with him in her home. Drew waits, unknowingly, for hours on her porch. At sunset, from the porch, Drew observes Lauren partially clothed in a heated embrace with her boyfriend. Very dejected, he looks on the scene and then wildly runs until he reaches the shore edge, only to encounter a similarly dejected Heather. They spend the night on the beach and make love off camera. The next day, they return to their respective homes. Heather kicks her philandering husband out of her house and life. Drew and his parents bid farewell to their relatives and return to their home. The film reconciles three central issues: Drew's emotional maturation, the intraracial–interfamilial class and political conflict between Kenny and Spencer, and the spiritual remarriage of Kenny and Brenda Tate.

This film offers a Frank Capra–like Hollywood ending in which marriage and society are seriously threatened but common sense and goodwill provide uplifting but simplistic narrative closure to very complex issues. *Soul Food* and *Eve's Bayou* are black-written and -directed family films that offer challenging narratives whose closures suggest no guarantees that moral or political storms will be resolved for all family members.

AS YOUNGER BLACK RAISINS SWEETEN IN THE SUN OF *SOUL FOOD* AND *EVE'S BAYOU*

The introspective voice-overs of the preteen Ahmad (Brandon Hammond) in *Soul Food* and Eve (Jurnee Smollett) in *Eve's Bayou* narrate certain transitional passages in each film. Similar to Drew in *The Inkwell*, Ahmad and Eve are the youngest members of their respective families and are the major characters in each film. Unlike seventeen-year-old Drew, Ahmad offers unbiased observations that show compassion for all family members, regardless of a passing deceitful action. Contrary to Ahmad's amoral attitude, Drew actively scrutinizes public morality. He becomes Heather's avenging angel and conspires against her husband's philandering. Ironically, when he realizes that Lauren Kelly has used him, he makes love to Heather, the very woman whose marriage he was trying to save. In *Soul Food*, Ahmad's motivation works toward the harmonious reestablishment of the extended family and acknowledges that the adulterous members and those they hurt will not be fully forgiven. *The Inkwell*'s closure brings harmony to the familial conflicts that introduced the film. In *Eve's Bayou*, however, Eve begins the film with "Memory is a selection of images, some elusive, others imprinted on the brain. The summer I killed my father I was ten years old." These words describe Eve's thoughts. She is more introspective than are most children of her age. Even Ahmad's voice-over monologues are not as poetic, in a Sylvia Plath–like manner, as the introspective Eve's. Still, *Eve's Bayou* is not a story about a prepubescent girl's plan to kill her father.

Soul Food begins at the wedding celebration of the youngest of three daughters. Ahmad's voice-over introduces the members of his family while a family photo album provides portraits of each member with their character and actor names. There is the matriarch Big Mama (Irma P. Hall), who for forty years has cooked a Sunday dinner for the family. She and her now-deceased husband migrated to Chicago from Mississippi. In attendance are her three biological daughters: Teri (Vanessa Williams), a lawyer and the eldest; Maxine (Vivica A. Fox), a homemaker and mother of three; and Bird (Nia Long), a beautician and the youngest. Accompanying her daughters are their respective husbands, Miles (Michael Beach), a disenchanted lawyer; Kenny (Jeffrey D. Sams), a blue-collar worker; and Lem (Mekhi Phifer), an unemployed ex-convict. Maxine and Kenny's three children, Ahmad (Brandon Hammond), Kelly (Morgan Méchelle Smith), and later a newborn child, make up only part of this extended family. The other members include Faith (Gina Ravera), a twenty-something relative whom Big Mama raised as her adopted daughter; Reverend Williams (Carl Wright), the recurrent Sunday dinner guest; and Uncle Pete (John M. Watson Sr.), who lives in the house but only appears at the film's end.

The exposition scene presents a broad spectrum of individuals who form a typical African American family. The marriage party hints that adultery and the incarceration of black men will threaten the stability of this family. The initial scene introduces all family members with the

The last supper of the matron and the momentary dissolution of the family (the adults from left to right): Carl Wright as Reverend Williams, Vanessa L. Williams as Teri, Jeffrey D. Sams as Kenny, Vivica A. Fox as Maxine, Irma P. Hall as Big Mama, Gina Ravera as Faith, Nia Long as Bird, Mekhi Phifer as Lem, and Michael Beach as Miles in George Tillman Jr.'s *Soul Food* (1997). (20th Century Fox / The Kobal Collection / Hodes, Charles)

exception of Faith and Uncle Pete. Teri, the most educated and profes-
sionally successful of Big Mama's girls, pays for the cost of Bird's wedding
party and furnishes the money that maintains Big Mama's house in its
good condition. Only Big Mama, Uncle Pete, Bird, and Lem live in the
roomy two-story house located in a middle-class African American
neighborhood on Chicago's Southside.

The narrative presents a sensitive portrait of Lem, Bird's ex-convict
husband. Throughout the film, he seeks employment but is unsuccessful.
Lem's first employer fires him after discovering that Lem has lied on the
job application. Lem responded "no" to the question about whether he
had any prior criminal convictions. On his next job applications, Lem
tells the truth, only to receive rejections from all prospective employers.
Bird persuades Simuel St. James (Mel Jackson), her ex-boyfriend, to get
Lem hired at the firm where Simuel has an $80,000 executive position.
Simuel acquiesces to Bird's request and expects that his efforts will rekin-
dle their past romance, but Bird is married to Lem in her heart and mind
and does not share Simuel's feeling. In an effort to destroy Bird's marriage, Simuel informs Lem how Bird had requested his assistance in getting Lem hired. In a fit of jealousy and shame, Lem punches Simuel to
the floor and kicks him. Simuel calmly fires Lem. An enraged and humil-
iated Lem bursts into Bird's beauty parlor and confronts her. He roughs
her up in the backroom, and she is brought to tears. Teri, the eldest sister,
who financed Bird's shop, arrives and enlists her ex-convict cousin Blimp
(Theron Touché Lykes) to teach Lem a lesson. In a neighborhood bar,
Lem is trying to drown his hurt when Blimp and his two associates enter.
The two associates strike Lem, who though intoxicated, punches Blimp's
two sidekicks and pulls a gun on Blimp. The police arrive and take all
four men into custody.

In a subsequent scene, Teri returns home to discover her husband
Miles having sex with her stepsister Faith. Because she is with her
nephew Ahmad, Teri controls her anger for Ahmad's sake. She quickly
takes Ahmad out of her house. When Miles arrives at Maxine and Kenny's party in celebration of eleven years of marriage, Teri dispenses with
her usual self-restraint and allows her emotions to guide her. Brandishing
a carving knife, Teri goes after Miles and screams obscenities at Faith.
Luckily, Kenny restrains Teri, who screams "Faith fucked my husband."
All sisters and guests behold Teri in a rare instance when she is hysterical.
Like all present, she does have feelings. Teri feels that she is entitled to
the respect of all her sisters because she has financed her younger sister's
business, maintained Big Mama's house, and paid the bills when her

mother needed an operation. Another instance that shows a more sensitive Teri occurs when guilt and remorse provoke her to enlist yet another friend, who gets Lem released from his already four weeks of imprisonment.

This family film is black scripted, directed, and produced. It features female characters in most of the narrative space and, except for male characters Lem and Ahmad, the women have the more important roles. Still, the narrative tends to honor mainstream moral and aesthetic norms that vilify Teri, a twice-married, very successful lawyer. It performs a similar function for Faith, the unmarried modern dancer who is successful in neither her career nor her love life. Ironically, Teri has a successful career and a horrible marriage that Faith, her nemesis and diametric opposite, will help to destroy. Teri's experience with marriage is a second attempt. In the conventional sense, couples marry to have children. Teri and Miles are the only childless married couple. The marital norm condemns their marriage as fruitless and furthers such condemnation by making the husband an adulterer. Contrastingly, Maxine is happily married to Kenny, Teri's childhood boyfriend. Maxine is thrice a mother, and Teri's youngest sister Bird is also lovingly married, as newlyweds can be, and pregnant. Teri and Faith are physically appealing, but they are the least likable persons in this extended family. Teri is an antiheroic example of an upper-class, ambitious black woman. She exemplifies the contemporary and generally circulated stereotype of a female who has a successful career and a failing marriage in which the "sensitive" husband becomes an adulterer when he rightly seeks a more sensitive female. In a more classical way, Faith typifies the black femme fatale as performed by such black actors as Lena Horne and Dorothy Dandridge. Female protagonists of this type are antithetical to family film because they are evil incarnate—the bad girls. In this particular film, the bad girls are Teri and Faith. They lack the maternal ingredients that make good, nurturing soul food that births black babies and keeps black men at home. The film circulates caricatures and demonizes the two childless, middle-class women. Judicious but young Ahmad, however, works against the narrative's conventional reading, which separates good women and men from their bad sisters and brothers. He offers a womanist postNegritude entreaty for Faith, Miles, Lem, and Teri to pay homage to a forty-year-old tradition in which the family gathers to enjoy Sunday dinner. This image closes the film. The tradition and family are preserved after such threats as Big Mama's death in the hospital, Miles and Faith's adultery, the dissolution of Teri's marriage, and Lem's jailing and release. Ahmad reassures the stoic Teri, the adulterers Faith and Miles, and the ex-convict Lem that they are still members of this family and must act in accordance.

Eve's Bayou is set in the 1960s in a black Louisiana community that has high regard for the charming Louis Batiste (Samuel L. Jackson), a family doctor who is renowned throughout the town for his womanizing. Even his wife, the beautiful Roz Batiste (Lynn Whitfield), is aware of his extramarital affairs and grudgingly permits them. Louis and Roz have two young daughters—Cisely (Meagan Good), the oldest child, and ten-year-old Eve (Jurnee Smollett)—and a son named Poe (Jake Smollett). The Batiste children, especially the girls, receive Louis's constant approving affections, which elude Roz. Similar to the townsfolk's expressed adoration for their doctor, the Batiste children worship their father but have mixed feelings for their black Southern belle of a mother, who is always impeccably dressed and reserved when in the company of her peers. It seems odd that the town does not censor Louis for his womanizing, which shames his wife, whose public stature is honorable.

The Batistes are an aristocratic black family. They live in a very spacious Victorian-style house that opens onto a large wooded area. Though set in the South during the 1960s, this film does not have the conventional references to racism that are found in most black-oriented films with Southern settings. In this sense, *Eve's Bayou*'s Southern description resembles *The Inkwell*'s Northern representation of African American middle- to upper-middle-class life, portraying an exclusively black population that has little concern for what white America is doing.

Louis's womanizing makes him an insensitive, selfish, and worthless husband. Still, both daughters seek his attentions. Cisely, the eldest, adores him and awaits his nightly returns.

Roz has reconciled to be married to a man she no longer loves and has a growing hatred for. She does not push for a divorce and endures his sexual escapades to avoid bringing public shame on the Batiste family. This irks Eve, the youngest daughter, who has still not matured enough to understand the societal conventions that force a black Southern belle such as Roz to remain silent and endure. Eve rejects and condemns her mother's passivity and bribes her father into doing her bidding. She becomes more aware of the sham of her father's social prominence and increasingly faults him for mistreating her mother and, later, her sister. Eve's initial reaction to condemn and hold her father in moral contempt results from Cisely and Eve's rivalry for their father's affections. Since

Cisely is almost a teenager, with all its physical and psychological conno-
tations, she requests and receives more of Louis's paternal attentions than
the more psychologically mature Eve, who is a ten-year-old tomboy.

Eve finds solace when she visits Louis's sister, Mozelle Batiste Dela-
croix (Debbi Morgan), who provides Eve with maturity and insight.
Mozelle describes her life experiences, in which passion has ruled and
which always finish with the death or loss of the man she loves or has
married. Mozelle Batiste informs Eve that Louis Batiste has a similar
tragic fate in store.

Mozelle, a clairvoyant, has never given birth, though she has been
married and has had her share of lovers. Her trajectory resembles that of
Faith and Teri in *Soul Food*; all three are a type of black femme fatale, a
bad girl and the antithesis of the conventional female protagonist in family film. A womanist postNegritude analysis views these female characters
as acceptable options to womanhood. They are not aberrations of the
child-bearing, married woman norm. Accordingly, Mozelle, Faith, and
Teri exist not as deformations or even as alternatives, but rather as one of
many acceptable options. If we extend this to the pubescent Eve and
Cisely, and the adult Roz, we discover that Eve is closer to Mozelle, Teri,
and Faith than she is to the conventional good girls, Cisely, Roz, and the
two sisters Maxine and Bird in *Soul Food*. Eve's voice-over is what makes
the black bayou magical and female centered within a narrative world
where wide-ranging female types tell their stories. The bonding between
Mozelle and Eve is like Big Mama's traditional Sunday dinners—both
bring family together, and sometimes the family is an exchange between
two wise women, one young and one older with more stories to tell. It
follows that after this womanist exchange, Eve will be able to witness a
very traumatic and destructive experience.

Late one night after too much drinking, Louis returns and finds
Cisely waiting for him. In his drunken confusion, he allows Cisely to sit
on his lap and, thinking his daughter to be his wife Roz, becomes pas-
sionately aroused. Louis caresses Cisely as he has not done with his wife
for some time. He sees Roz in Cisely and proceeds to make love to this
imagined Roz. He awakens from his drunken stupor before completing
his incestuous destruction of Cisely, the only family member who
admires him. *Eve's Bayou* explores the developing independent personal-
ity of Eve, who, like Ahmad in *Soul Food*, is the youngest and the pro-
vider of a womanist vision that, in postNegritude, is available for women
and men. *Eve's Bayou* presents a stoic form of womanism because it

The youngest daughter learns to love and respect her mother, who endures a philandering husband: Jurnee Smollett as Eve Batiste and Lynn Whitfield as Roz Batiste in Kasi Lemmons's *Eve's Bayou* (1997). (Trimark Pictures / The Kobal Collection)

denies *The Inkwell*'s utopian and simple-minded dénouement. Similarly, it resists *Soul Food*'s measured utopian image, which acknowledges familial problems and is willing to live with them for the preservation of the whole collective. *Eve's Bayou* does not have a comfortable place for adulterers such as Eve's father Louis Batiste, Harold (*The Inkwell*), Miles and Faith (*Soul Food*), and the callous, upper-class black professionals Spencer (*The Inkwell*) and Teri (*Soul Food*).

KASI LEMMONS'S PREPRODUCTION WOMANIST AGENCY IN *EVE'S BAYOU*

Kasi Lemmons's *Eve's Bayou* presents a particular type of black female–centered family film that employs magical realism, unlike her second feature, *Caveman's Valentine* (Jersey Films, 2001), which tells the story of a father–daughter relationship. Also included in this magical-realist, family-film subgenre are Charles Burnett's *To Sleep with Anger* and John Singleton's *Rosewood*, especially in each film's use of African American mythology and magical imagery. The elements of black mythology, folk religion, and heroic legends combine to dramatize how black middle-class families in Los Angeles, New Orleans, and Rosewood, Florida, endure threats to the family unit.

Kasi Lemmons's discussion of how she brought her script to the screen conveys the difficulties faced by any black woman writer–director who seeks Hollywood studios' financing or distribution.

Similar to *Eve's Bayou*'s innovative womanist narrative elements, the film's production history contains a black female–interested narrative. Referring to the preproduction discussions with studio executives concerning the script she wrote for *Eve's Bayou*, Lemmons described how production executives tried to make her revise her script to include at least one white racist. A racist white is an omnipresent and all-powerful villain in Hollywood's conventional Southern imagery. Lemmons noticed that "the really interesting thing with *Eve's Bayou* is that studio people would ask me to put in white characters. I mean, even if they were negative white characters—just any white character. They would say, 'Can't there be a racist?' And I just said, 'This is *Eve's Bayou*.'"[1] In the same interview, Lemmons considered the importance of contracting a known star to attract studio funding, but this did not guarantee the studio's total commitment to the project. She explained, "When I was trying to make *Eve's Bayou*, the studios would say, 'Oh we love it. It's a beautiful script. But you need to get a star. If you could get, say, Sam Jackson.' Sam's people read the script, and we attached him to the project. Then we went back to those same studio people and said, 'We got Sam Jackson,' and they were like 'Oh. You got him. We didn't really mean that.' Even with Sam attached, in both these cases—it's not a piece of cake, because the subject matter is not mainstream."[2] Lemmons stated, "As soon as you get an agent, [the agent] warns you. I remember one time I was trying to sell *Eve's Bayou*, and I was talking to this executive. At a certain point, he said that there was a part of the script he didn't get. I did not suck my teeth or anything like that, but I did sit back and cross my arms. I got a lecture about it afterwards. I was told to never sit back and cross your arms, because now these people think you're a bitch. There's something about black women that frightens people. People are waiting for you to be kind of bitter."[3] She continued and discussed the broader issue of women directing and writing films for mainstream studios. "I find that women—as filmmakers and as people—are not interested in putting up with the status quo. Most of the women I know are aware of the deepness of women. There are many white male filmmakers who have captured women beautifully, and, of course, there are works of literature in which women have been beautifully realized by men. But in cinema we're just not seeing it, for some reason, in regard to black women. One of the things that motivated me to make *Eve's Bayou* the way I did was that I was sick of the image of the noble, slightly sweaty, angry black woman. I remember after I did *Eve's Bayou*, someone said, 'You were in Louisiana—why weren't those women sweating?' I said, 'You know what? I've had enough sweaty people.' I just didn't want to see any sweat. I wasn't feeling that. I was feeling this other thing that I experienced in my youth, looking at my family and my neighbors and the people that I knew—this beauty and glamour."[4] Chapter 5 focuses on this general issue, analyzes the dramatic limitations of the black female lead and supporting actress in 1990s films, and highlights selected films that feature Whoopi Goldberg and Halle Berry as lead or supporting actors.

Lemmons distinguishes the problems that the female writer–director generally experiences from the particular problems faced by black women. Black women in Hollywood encounter a double-edged sword when pitching black-oriented female-centered scripts such as *Eve's Bayou*. The black woman writer–director must consistently argue for stories that faithfully represent black female experiences that seem unimportant to Hollywood studios' conception of mainstream audience tastes. Thus, the black woman writer–director's ability to successfully obtain major studio funding and distribution of her films is doubly difficult. Still, as discussed later in chapter 5, major and mini-major studios have successfully produced and distributed a small number of black female–centered films. Lemmons concludes her interview with a confident attitude and mentions the large number of women who worked on *Eve's Bayou* and *The Caveman's Valentine*'s production crews. She believes that women will increasingly occupy technical positions in the film industry. "I feel strongly about women. Both of my movies have had an extraordinary number of women working on them. This last movie [*The Caveman's Valentine*], all my keys were women—the DP, the producer, the editor, the production designer. On *Eve's Bayou,* it was the same thing. I think that *that* is important for the industry. It's opening up. It's going to happen. It's inevitable. Even if they didn't want it to happen, it's going to happen. It's a wave that's been set into motion."[5] More women in the film trade unions might ultimately translate into more women as writers and directors. Yet it does not necessarily translate into more women of color in various film unions as skilled technicians, writers, and filmmakers.

The Inkwell, Soul Food, and *Eve's Bayou* portray black middle-class extended families whose intrafamilial conflicts involve an individual's socioeconomic class standing or his/her past mistakes to which the film makes frequent allusions. Thus the black family films discussed in this chapter explore intergenerational conflicts between child and parent and class rivalry between the families' adult members. The three film narratives are mediated by a child or teenager's point of view, which matures as the film develops. Intergenerational and class conflicts are present in most family films that explore the social and psychological challenges of first-generation immigrant communities. Consequently, black family film shares narrative elements with other types of family films that dramatize issues concerning class mobility, social integration, and the effects of abandoning ethnic traditions and beliefs.

Black family films of the 1990s that dramatize urban poverty, adolescent delinquency, and the failing American justice system include Matty Rich's *Straight Out of Brooklyn,* John Singleton's *Boyz N the Hood* (Columbia Pictures, 1991), Ernest Dickerson's *Juice* (Paramount, 1992), Albert and Allen Hughes's *Menace II Society* (New Line Cinema, 1993), and Spike Lee's *Clockers* (Universal Pictures, 1995) and *He Got Game* (Touchstone Pictures, 1998). In their dramatization of black urban poverty, adolescent delinquency, and social injustice, these films show the unpleasant social reality of contemporary life in urban America. Contrastingly, other 1990s black family films such as *The Inkwell, Eve's Bayou,* and *Soul Food* show that, though racial discrimination and poverty exist in the African American community, their demoralizing effects are not always overwhelming as exemplified in Matty Rich's *Straight Out of Brooklyn*. Still, these three films point to contemporary problems that fracture the tenuous relationship between the upper middle class and the working and lower classes in the African American community. Certain blacks place more importance on the individual's responsibility for self-betterment than on the government's duty to guarantee the health and welfare of all its citizenry. The best of the black family films, such as *Crooklyn* (1994), *The Inkwell* (1994), *He Got Game* (1998), and *Soul Food* (1997), do not shirk their responsibility to dramatize the existence of class divisions in African American families. In their dramatization of interfamilial class discord, the films indicate a general problem in post–Civil Rights era America. They do not indicate an America that is now post-black or postracist. They point to the diverse political affinities, class differences, and individual experiences that exist in the postNegritude worldview.

NOTES

1. Ernest Hardy, "I, Too, Sing Hollywood: Four Women on Race, Art and Making Movies," *L.A. Weekly,* 20–26, October 2000, at www.laweekly.com/ink/00/48/cover-hardy1.shtml.
2. Hardy, "I, Too, Sing Hollywood."
3. Hardy, "I, Too, Sing Hollywood."
4. Hardy, "I, Too, Sing Hollywood."
5. Hardy, "I, Too, Sing Hollywood."

· *3* ·

Black Action Film after Twenty Years

$\mathscr{T}$he black action-film genre—for the purposes of this discussion—includes films that focus on black characters as cowboys, soldiers, police officers, detectives, spies, gangsters, bank robbers, drug dealers, and anyone else involved in espionage or illegal activities. The black action film is any film whose narrative features any of these types of characters in major or secondary roles and whose central action is set in the black community. Here I survey mostly black gangster films because this subgenre has a long and rich history that covers the early period of black film production to the 1990s. It also reflects both unique and conventional film treatments in its representation of race, urban poverty, masculinity, and violence.

A look at the depiction of criminality in early "race films" provides some useful background. The term "race film" refers to all-black-cast films that small independent film companies produced for the African American audience from 1912 to the 1940s. Race films were usually exhibited in movie theaters frequented by African Americans or in white theaters that were rented for racially segregated exhibitions to black audiences. This chapter offers an interpretation of two early black gangster films that established two types of black film crime narratives. It then moves to a general examination of black action films and their subgenres spanning from the 1970s to the present.

GANGSTERS IN BLACK INDEPENDENT FILM

The subject of race and the construction of the racial subject in popular media and the social and biological sciences continues to be a much-

37

shunned topic. The way in which we describe "blacks" resembles the problems we encounter when attempting a monolithic description of Jews, Muslims, and Christians. Any attempt to describe these subject identities provokes volatile disagreements between scholars and laypersons, regardless of their race, ethnicity, or political hue. One need only recall the debate over the term *biracial* and the burden faced by any biracial celebrities when asked about their racial identity. Nevertheless, I offer a tentative description of the representation of "race" and "blacks" in genre film. My postNegritude description holds that "race" and "blacks" are ever-changing sociocultural constructions. Sometimes, national boundaries and local political factors redefine what constitutes the racial or black subject. Rather than biological and genetically assigned characteristics, "race" and "black folk" are sociological categories. Furthermore, the sociohistorical moment determines the contours of the representation of race. Previously, scholars have avoided writing about the representation of race in genre film. In pre–Rodney King/Reginald Denny America, the socioeconomic status of African Americans did not immediately affect film scholarship. Equally true, in pre–Anita Hill America the importance of black women confronting sexual harassment in the workplace was of little concern to mainstream feminism. The Republican Party's use of the black rapist Willie Horton during the 1988 presidential campaign, the 1991 videotaped beatings of Rodney King and Reginald Denny, the Anita Hill–Clarence Thomas 1991 Senate hearing, and the O. J. Simpson murder trial forced conscientious media and feminist scholars to pay closer attention to the visual construction of the racial subject, male and female.[1]

Recent articles that discuss the representation of race in black gangster films have narrowed their survey to discuss such trendy gangsta rap films as John Singleton's *Boyz N the Hood* (Columbia Pictures, 1991), Mario Van Peebles's *New Jack City* (Warner Brothers, 1991), and Ernest Dickerson's *Juice* (Paramount, 1992). Consequently, these scholars inadvertently suggest that there exists no history or tradition for black gangster films. Film journalism once had a secure place in the academy, but advances in film study have made it easy to reject this form of popular journalistic writing about film.[2]

Most important, the typical black gangster film shares the contemporary narrative conventions and iconography of the mainstream Hollywood gangster movie. For the most part, African American moviegoers who enjoy gangster films are entertained by the same outlaw fantasies as

Jermaine Hopkins as Steel, Omar Epps as Q, Tupac Shakur as Bishop, and Khalil Kain as Raheem in Ernest Dickerson's *Juice* (1992). (Island World / The Kobal Collection)

white moviegoers. The sole difference between the two audiences bears on the racial and sociocultural elements that construct the gangster hero(ine). Genre conventions and audience expectations demand that black gangsters perform similar feats. One might ask, then, why even study the black gangster film if it is only a second-rate imitation of Hollywood fare?

Even though most imaginative portrayals of African American criminal life borrow mainstream narrative conventions and iconography, there are certain black gangster films that evoke a markedly ethnic-inflected difference. For instance, a particular noncriminal segment of the black community may condone certain illegal activities, while certain middle-class individuals in the same community may denounce them. Such a culturally marked difference in the construction of "law and order" results from sociocultural divisions within and without the African American community. Such an experience, however, does not reflect a biological or racial fact.

This book neither argues for a biological determinist aesthetic construction of blackness nor supports the belief that racial experience determines the formal elements of a film practice. In outlining a short history of the black action film and its subgenres, this chapter shows how the representation of race resists certain narrative conventions that support a strict definition of "law and order" and a monolithic definition of "blackness."

Any analysis of the history of black film and its political nature should consider who produces and distributes these films. Interpretations should describe how blacks have surreptitiously controlled the financing and distribution of their films or, more important, should reveal how blacks avoided the disemboweling effects of studio decisions and censorship board rulings. If analysis does not consider both the creative and the industrial aspects of black filmmaking, then research will further mask the determining factors that inhibit the production of black independent films.

Agents of culture have selected the group of extant race films and the commerce that has financed, distributed, or archived particular films. These agents inadvertently permit the disappearance of certain black-oriented films while they design the boundaries of what critics can accurately discuss based on their review of these films. Therefore, when critical attention is directed at race films, the critic must recognize the various selective processes that these films have undergone. Early black film history is a story of omissions as well as a tale of inclusions.

As early as 1926, Oscar Micheaux wrote and directed *Spider's Web*—which documents the numbers racket, an organized form of gambling prevalent in certain urban communities. The following year, Frank Peregini directed the David Starkman screenplay *The Scar of Shame* (Colored Players Film Corp., 1927). This film describes a racially dualistic world in which socioeconomic factors create the "good black" as an assimilated, whitened Negro and the "bad nigger" as true to his or her primitive nature. *The Scar of Shame*'s depiction of black middle-class mobility supports a Manichaean view of America as a racially dualistic system. Confined to the determinants of this system, according to the narrative logic of *The Scar of Shame*, African American socioeconomic success requires that blacks either adopt European standards or accept their essential "bad nigger" nature. According to this dualistic system, the more unfortunate blacks must use their natural "bad nigger" ways to survive in the ghetto streets, middle-class blacks have somehow suppressed the black gangster self to become assimilated, while the black criminal has made good use of his or her "natural" criminal character. Thus it is better to be true to one's black criminal genes than to assimilate and suppress an essentially devilish and primitive nature. The film's portrayal of black criminality as biologically determined is, of course, flawed. In rejecting the film's biological determinist portrait, historian Thomas Cripps writes:

> The picture placed the black thrust for "the finer things" against the drag of the coarse, grinding ghetto that cheats the hero of beauty and virtue. . . . The hard world of the streets makes brutes and hustlers of smart blacks with a will to live. They are the inassimilable "bad niggers" who can never leave the darkened doorways of the ghetto demimonde, but whose guile permits them to survive in cool style. Unfortunately, the picture stumbles when it asks the Negro to rise above the life of the streets because it draws a veil over the external forces that made the slum what it is. Thus, the hero . . . can end his suffering only by opting for white culture and rejecting black.[3]

The narrative closure of *The Scar of Shame* reflects the cultural period of the Harlem Renaissance and the economic necessity to please the white patrons of black art. During the 1920s, the psychological well-being of white middle-class urbanites rested on the ability of black performers to satiate the primitive fantasies of the paying audience. For instance, there is the image of Josephine Baker in her banana dress revealing the backside of this performer and providing her white audience with the unholy juju of one of their most primitive obsessions.

Although Micheaux's *Harlem after Midnight* (1934) developed a thicker sociocultural description of black organized crime, the film sustained the color-caste system and Manichaean moral choices found in *The Scar of Shame*. Micheaux's ability to imitate his successful white contemporary Josef von Sternberg is apparent in *Underworld* (1937). Ten years before Micheaux's 1937 lensing of *Underworld*, Paramount Studios released von Sternberg's *Underworld* (1927). Von Sternberg's film is the first, and perhaps one of the best, examples of the classic American gangster film. Like the many other directors of gangster films who followed von Sternberg's *Underworld*, Micheaux borrowed narrative devices from von Sternberg's 1927 silent masterpiece. Both films portray an innocent young man's ascendance through the ranks of crime that culminates with the young gangster's spiritual and physical possession of the former crime boss's girlfriend. In the classic gangster narrative, the rightful heir of the mob boss deposes the reigning paternal order. The hero takes possession of the objects that had once validated his boss's entrepreneurial skill and sexual prowess. The objects include the former mob boss's territory, the henchmen, the material tokens of wealth, and his girlfriend. The territory of the crime family includes the gang leader's girl, and thus the classical gangster film narrative generates patriarchal rights of succession.

Micheaux's *Underworld* borrows several gangster film elements from von Sternberg's film of the same title. Micheaux's film shows how a Southern black college graduate moves to Chicago, falls into a life of crime, and rises through the ranks of a black-controlled crime organization. Micheaux's narrative presents Chicago's socioeconomic conditions as a major factor in the moral decay of an educated Southern black youth. In von Sternberg's film, black gangsters and the black community are totally absent, unless they appear as local color and background props.

FROM INDEPENDENT STUDIO TO
MAJOR HOLLYWOOD STUDIOS

In 1937, Ralph Cooper and George Randol, two African Americans, and Ben Rinaldo, a white American, organized the Cooper-Randol Production Company in Los Angeles. The same year, Cooper and Harry Fraser's *Dark Manhattan* (Cooper-Randol Production Company, 1937) became the first all-black-cast gangster film made in Hollywood.[4] The film dramatizes a man's rise in the numbers racket, his love for a nightclub singer, and his death at the hands of a rival mobster. The Cooper-Randol film company was short-lived and produced only one film; Ralph Cooper left the company and established Million Dollar Productions with Harry and Leo Popkin, two white Americans. Cooper wrote and sometimes directed, while the Popkin brothers financed and distributed Cooper's films.[5] Their first such collaboration was *Bargain with Bullets* (Million Dollar Productions, 1937), which Cooper wrote, directed, and starred in.[6] The following year, Cooper wrote *Gang Smashers* (Million Dollar Productions, 1938), which featured Nina Mae McKinney as a Harlem crime boss (almost ten years earlier, McKinney had performed the leading role of Chick in King Vidor's black musical *Hallelujah!* [MGM, 1929]). In the film *Gang War* (Million Dollar Productions, 1939), Cooper portrayed a mobster who struggles unsuccessfully for control over the jukebox machines in Harlem. *Gang War* was Cooper's last film for the Popkin brothers' Million Dollar Productions.

Cooper's departure from Million Dollar Productions coincided with the Popkins' forming an exclusive sales distribution contract with Sack Amusement Enterprise of Dallas. From the early 1920s through the 1940s, Sack Amusement was the leading distributor of race films because it entered into deals with production companies and theaters that catered to the African American market.[7] In Cooper's last gangster film, *Am I Guilty?* (Supreme Pictures, 1940), he played a naïve doctor whose clinic was surreptitiously financed and controlled by a mobster. *Gang War* and *Am I Guilty?* explored the demise of a black protagonist who loses control over his business. Henry Sampson writes that "Ralph quit Million Dollar Productions in 1939 because he was tired of playing gangster type roles."[8] Nevertheless, I suspect that Cooper's last two films dramatize the unequal power relationship he had with the Popkin brothers. Cooper was a copartner in the firm, an actor in its films, and a writer–director of several Million Dollar Productions. Obviously, he enjoyed some creative freedoms, but he lacked decisive control over the extent to which the company financed and distributed his creative work. One can speculate that because the Popkins controlled the financing, distribution, and exhibition of Cooper's films, they probably forced a too-ambitious Cooper to seek employment elsewhere.

Although Oscar Micheaux's contribution to the development of black gangster films was important, it was Ralph Cooper's codirection and starring role in the 1937 *Dark Manhattan* that introduced a primarily Northern-based story about black gangster life. Micheaux was one of the first to feature a black gangster in a major role. The director–actor Ralph Cooper, however, developed the Northern, urban, black gangster film style. This type of black gangster figured in the cycle of 1970s black action films such as Gordon Parks Jr.'s *Superfly* (Warner Brothers, 1972) and John Evans's *The Black Godfather* (Cinemation, 1974), revived in *New Jack City* (Warner Brothers, 1991).

Veteran African American stage and screen performers such as the actor–writers Frank Wilson and Ralph Cooper and the actresses Edna Mae Harris and Nina Mae McKinney appeared in several of the earliest all-black-cast gangster films—*Harlem after Midnight, Underworld, Dark Manhattan, Bargain with Bullets, Gang Smashers, Gang War, Paradise in Harlem* (Goldberg Productions, 1939), and *Murder on Lenox Avenue* (Goldberg Productions, 1941).

During the 1930s, a few Hollywood crime films featured interracial groups of criminals. For example, Edward Thompson appears as a police lieutenant in *Bargain with Bullets* (1937), a gangster in Arthur Dreifuss's *Double Deal* (International Road Show, 1939), a lawyer in *Am I Guilty?* (Supreme Pictures, 1940), and again as a gangster in *The Petrified Forest* (1936), directed by Archie Mayo. Louise Beavers, the mammy figure in many Hollywood films, performs maternal roles in her two race films— *Life Goes On* (Million Dollar Productions, 1938) and *Reform School* (Million Dollar Productions, 1939). The Hollywood gangster film *Bullets or Ballots* (Warner Brothers, 1936), directed by William Keighley, features Edward G. Robinson, Humphrey Bogart, Joan Blondell, and Beavers as Madame Nellie La Fleur, the boss of a Harlem numbers racket. Because both *Bullets or Ballots* and the all-black-cast *Gang Smashers* feature a black woman as boss of the Harlem crime world, one might surmise that the female mobster role was a popular novelty in films of the period.

In American crime films since the 1960s, black lawmen have been members of governmental policing agencies. For example, Virgil Tibbs (Sidney Poitier) of *In the Heat of the Night* (directed by Norman Jewison, UA, 1967) and Axel Foley (Eddie Murphy) of *Beverly Hills Cop* (directed by Martin Brest, Paramount, 1984) are police officers, while John Shaft (Richard Roundtree) of *Shaft* (directed by Gordon Parks Sr., MGM, 1971) is a state-licensed private detective. In black-cast gangster films of the post–Civil Rights period, blacks portray police officers and federal agents. Major motion pictures of the 1930s and 1940s, however, rarely featured blacks as licensed agents of the law. Many 1930s and 1940s films depict figures of lawful authority in roles as community leaders and paternal figures. A few of these race films generate established ideas of "law and order." On viewing some of them, one can trace how different belief systems organize and police the black community. I shall discuss how two 1940s black gangster films, *Murder on Lenox Avenue* and Powell Lindsay's *Souls of Sin* (Alexander Productions, 1949), generate different ideas about "race" and the construction of the gangster figure.

The morally upright characters tend to espouse a traditional understanding of "law and order." The agents of the law are neither officially recognized nor licensed by state institutions, as are Virgil Tibbs, Axel Foley, and John Shaft. Thus analysis must consider how the imagined black community authorizes its leaders and, in turn, how leaders, or other narrative forces, rid the community of gangsters. The community leader as unlicensed policing agent, and the black gangster as innate villain, reflect the conventional gangster paradigm in *Murder on Lenox Avenue*.

A Northern African American big city cop teams up with a white Southern small town police chief, and the two law officers make history: Sidney Poitier as detective Virgil Tibbs and Rod Steiger as Police Chief Bill Gillespie in Norman Jewison's *In the Heat of the Night* (1967). (Mirisch/United Artists / The Kobal Collection)

The film illustrates how a gangster narrative incorporates a conservative view of "law and order." Pa Wilkins, the film's major protagonist, is a single parent and respected member of the Harlem business community. Ola Wilkins, Pa's daughter, is a schoolteacher who wants to leave Harlem and help Frank, her boyfriend, educate black children in the South. Both Ola and Pa respect the principles of civic duty and personal honesty, and the value that education has for the advancement of the race. Pa, however, disagrees with Ola's plans to move to the South. He would prefer that Ola remain in Harlem, forget Frank, and marry Jim Branston, Pa's adopted son whose deceased father was Pa's army friend. Unknown to Pa Wilkins, Jim has been sexually active with the now-pregnant daughter of Pa's cleaning lady. Branston rejects his paternal responsibility for the pregnancy because Pa has promised him Ola to wed and her trust fund when Pa dies. Rejecting her father's wishes, Ola marries Frank, and the two leave for the South. This provokes a momentary rupture in the Wilkins family.

Additionally, Pa Wilkins must rectify the financial problems that plague the Harlem Better Business League. Marshall, the League's president, has persuaded the League's membership to buy expensive equipment on credit. Later, the members discover that the monthly credit payments are draining their cash reserves. The Harlem Better Business League is Pa's second family, a community, and a business family. Consequently, Pa must remedy Marshall's recklessness, which occasions a second family rupture. Pa corrects the problem by unseating Marshall as the League's president.

Marshall is unable to accept this public loss, however, and arranges for one of his henchmen to murder Pa Wilkins. He also enlists Jim Branston, who reluctantly accepts, after recognizing that Pa's death will permit the distribution of Ola's trust fund. Marshall's first attempt at murder fails. When Ola and Frank read about the attempt on Pa's life, they depart from the South and rush to his aid. Ola's return reunites the Wilkins family, but Pa must still correct the financial problems that threaten the Harlem Better Business League. Finally, when gangsters make a second attempt on Pa's life, narrative forces of "law and order" prevail. Jim Branston tries to save Pa from a bullet fired by Marshall's henchman and receives the fatal shot. The police arrest Marshall and his gunman. The reunited Wilkins family and Pa's presidency of the Harlem Better Business League celebrate paternal order, righteousness, and Christian redemption. Jim's altruistic action and death are penance for the abandonment of his pregnant lover and her ensuing suicide. Furthermore, Jim's move to save Pa restores his loyalty to Pa Wilkins, a paternal figure of moral order. Moreover, Jim's death permits a morally upright and civic-minded couple, Ola and Frank, to continue Pa Wilkins's work and inherit his legacy.

The film's narrative reconstitutes Pa Wilkins's private family and public responsibility, which reflects a rather patriarchal understanding of "law and order." Pa Wilkins is "father" to the Harlem-based Better Business League; he is "Pa" to Ola and her mate; and he is the adoptive father of Branston, the man who gives his life for the betterment of the whole community. The film's seamless moral code and narrative thus construct Pa Wilkins as an unlicensed policing agent.

Similar to the construction of evil in the morality play, *Murder on Lenox Avenue* does not attempt to justify or explain Marshall's criminality. His baseness is both naturalized and fixed in his handsome physiognomy, in his neat urban dress, and in his amoral determination to control his social environment. *Murder on Lenox Avenue* borrows the moral logic of the conventional gangster film and presents a simplistic image of criminality as a genetically fixed trait. Consequently, we do not know why Marshall pursues a life of crime.

In the late 1940s, one film attempted to dramatize why an individual might turn to crime to advance his socioeconomic position. Progressive African Americans produced, wrote, and directed *Souls of Sin* (1948), a film that portrays how daunted hopes lead to a life of crime. Similarly to Richard Wright's argument in *Native Son* (1940), *Souls of Sin* portrays how social factors, not the inherent disposition of the individual, produce criminals.

Souls of Sin dramatizes the lives of three men who live in a Harlem rooming house. Each roomer has a special dream of success. Roberts, a middle-aged writer and paternal figure, hopes to gain employment as a writer, but publishers have consistently rejected his stories. Yet he continues typing his tales and cherishes the hope that some press will publish his work. He maintains an authorial distance from what he refers to as "the jungle." Dollar Bill is a well-dressed and embittered gambler who maintains a sufficient amount of self-pity. Bill's misguided pride fuels a desire to regain his former status as a neighborhood celebrity. Unable to win fame as a successful gambler, he joins a burglary gang led by Bad Boy George. As a gang member, Bill transports and sells stolen goods. Dollar Bill, like Jim Branston in *Murder on Lenox Avenue*, is a prodigal son. His social experiences in Manhattan have dehumanized him; yet, unlike Jim's disrespect for Pa Wilkins, Dollar Bill shows a sincere kindness toward his two roommates, the elderly Roberts and the youthful Alabama. Alabama, the third roommate, has recently arrived from Alabama. He is a naïve but promising youth. He is new to New York and therefore has not run across the professional obstacles that keep Roberts punching away at a typewriter and Bill dodging the police. Unlike Dollar Bill, Alabama is satisfied with a commonplace life playing music. His patience rewards him with employment playing his guitar and singing the blues, and he is quick to achieve fame. The relationship among these three men resembles that of a motherless family in which Roberts, like Pa Wilkins, is the paternal figure and spiritual adviser.

Both *Murder on Lenox Avenue* and *Souls of Sin* reflect familial bonding in which mothers are absent. Both films portray Harlem nightclub life and feature black vaudeville acts. Yet these similarities are insignificant because *Souls of Sin* focuses on the social environment that breeds criminality in the black community. The film begins with panoramic shots of the New York skyline and a voice-over narration that links these shots to a bird's-eye view of busy Harlem streets. Then the narration and the camera follow a solitary individual as he walks through the windy and cold streets. An eye-level long shot records a man briskly walking toward the camera and into the centrality of the film's visual and aural frames of reference.

The establishing shots inform us of the specific setting, New York's Harlem neighborhood. An eye-level long shot records a black man as he grasps his thin outer clothing, as he coolly walks toward the camera, and as he disappears into a tenement building. It is easy to assume that this man wants to avoid a gust of wind, to escape the socioeconomic forces that beat back his ever-so-cool movements. In language mixing poetic metaphors and social determinism, a narrator informs us:

> This is New York, as enchanting and imaginative as a dream. As romantic as moonlight on the ocean. As beautiful as fine sculpture. As ugly as this poverty-ridden slum. As warm and tender as a mother's love. . . . This is magnetic Manhattan. This is the story of souls lost in sin. . . . Caught in the panorama of this chaotic magnetic is one William Burton, alias Dollar Bill.

The introductory remarks in *Souls of Sin* generate compassion for Dollar Bill and disdain for the socioeconomic forces that lead him into a life of crime. The voice-over narrator argues for a special understanding of Harlem as "this poverty-ridden slum" that has caught William Burton in its magnet. Thus both the narrator and the film's initial documentary style construct Harlem as a social case study. The characters represent a vision of Harlem life that is consistent with the social-realist tone of the establishing shots at the film's outset.

At the end, a publisher commissions Roberts to write the story of Dollar Bill's life of crime. But Roberts does not see the importance of glamorizing Bill's criminality. He rejects the offer but agrees to write a story about the socioeconomic forces that produce criminals such as Bill. Roberts shares the social outlook of the voice-over narrator, a perspective that opens and closes the film.

In 1945, William Alexander, the producer of *Souls of Sin*, founded the Associated Film Producers of Negro Motion Pictures, Inc., a company that produced several black-oriented short documentaries and feature-length fiction films. Alexander's postwar films include *The Call of Duty* (1946) and *The Highest Tradition* (1946), short documentaries about black participation in the U.S. Navy and Army, respectively; *Flicker Up* (1946), a musical short that features Billy Eckstine and May Lou Harris; *Love in Syncopation* (1947), a feature film that dramatizes the story of "Henri Woods and his [jazz] band and their rise to fame from beginnings in the Seabees"[9] during black participation in World War II; *The Fight Never Ends* (1947), a feature depicting Joe Louis as himself fighting juvenile delinquency; *That Man of Mine* (1947), costarring Powell Lindsay and Ruby Dee; and *The Klansman* (1974), which Alexander coproduced, directed by Terence Young and starring Richard Burton, Lee Marvin, Lola Falana, and O. J. Simpson. Alexander's late 1940s productions and his collaboration with Powell Lindsay mark the end of black-controlled race film production companies. William Alexander shared the entrepreneurial interests of Oscar Micheaux, but also shared the social-realist interests of Powell Lindsay, the muse of black social realism on film.

Powell Lindsay, the writer and director of *Souls of Sin*, belonged to the short-lived Negro Playwrights Company. In 1940, he directed the company's first and last production, Theodore Ward's *The Big White Fog*. Lindsay's work reflects a cultural period when black social realism prevailed in the dramatic work of Theodore Ward, the fiction of Richard Wright, and the songs and speeches of Paul Robeson. A black social-realist ideology characterized the Negro Playwrights Company. One need only read the company's brochure, *A Professional Theatre with an Idea*, to understand that Powell Lindsay and his fellow members shared the viewpoint of the narrator of *Souls of Sin* and Roberts, a fictional character but authorial voice of Powell Lindsay. The brochure reads:

These new writers recognize that they live in a real society. . . . They will be writers worthy of the name, only if they remain independent of the forces which have reduced brains to a commodity, and driven weaklings and panderers to the practice of falsifying truth in order to make it conform to accepted beliefs, and the tastes of those who tend to regard the Negro people as children, or slaves placed in the world for their own exploitation or amusement.[10]

Souls of Sin is a fitting close to the black gangster film before the 1960s. The film and the people who collaborated to produce it prove that black gangster films can be socially conscious and entertaining while also instructing an audience.

Black gangster films, or films depicting black criminal elements, employ familiar criminal stock types, such as those found in African American literature. During the Civil Rights era, the novels of Holloway House writers Robert Beck (Iceberg Slim) and Donald Goines (Al C. Clark) created the most popular versions of black-oriented crime literature. The titles of their works create a typology of popular black criminals who appear in certain post-1960 black gangster films. Their Holloway House crime novels include such titles as Beck's *Pimp: The Story of My Life* (1967) and *Trick Baby* (1967; film version directed by Larry Yust, Universal Pictures, 1973) and Goines's *Dopefiend: The Story of a Black Junkie* (1971), *Whoreson: The Story of a Ghetto Pimp* (1972), and *Street Players* (1973).

A second group of black crime novels attracted the attention of literary scholars. These "canonical" works include Louise Meriwether's *Daddy Was a Number Runner* (1971), Robert Deane Pharr's *Book of Numbers* (1969; film version directed by Raymond St. Jacques for Avco-Embassy, 1973), and Chester Himes's *Cotton Comes to Harlem* (1965; film version directed by Ossie Davis for United Artists, 1970). Thieves, numbers runners, confidence men, drug dealers, and pimps form the cast of gangster types who populate the post-1960s black gangster family.

Individual gangsters employ professionals whose activities retain the veneer of respectability, though they may serve illegal purposes. For example, accountants, lawyers, politicians, and police officers are highly respected members of society, yet they sometimes have business connections with organized crime.

ORGANIZED CRIME AND ITS BLACK (DIS)CONTENTS

On the other side of the tracks are the criminal elements: hoodlums, drug dealers, pimps, and members of organized crime families. Audiences, regardless of their ethnic or racial makeup, recognize the requirements of a gangster film. They also are able to agree that certain actions are criminal, although they may differ on the moral issues surrounding these acts. This divergence of opinion might reflect any given audience's identification with the gangster. Because the film industry must adhere to censorship laws and depends on approval from the broadest audience of filmgoers, movie directors imitate successful gangster formulas and avoid controversial acts that would anger local censors and mainstream audiences.

A second aspect of this genre is its thematic elements. The treatments of certain social problems sometimes reflect the differences between the gangster films made by large studios such as Paramount and Warner Brothers and the black gangster films made by independent producers. This difference resembles the difference between organized crime and the random, anarchic criminal elements that exist outside a *legitimized* system of criminal production such as the mid-1980s savings and loan scandal or Irangate.[11]

By the late 1960s, black gangster films present black detectives and community leaders who are uneasy with their role as agents for governmental institutions of "law and order." Black gangster films do not reflect the moral vision of all members of the black community. An audience that constantly views these films must share a similar type of visual and psychic pleasure. This audience might identify with the gangster's adventurous life, material possessions, and sexual prowess. The audience momentarily identifies with the gangster's acts of violence as he unseats his rivals and evades the law. Audiences relish his unwavering ability to garner the love of women without reciprocating. Gangster films celebrate individual fortitude and aggrandizing greed. Only the gangster's capture awakens one from this amoral daydream and thereby reestablishes the monotony of the moral majority within the film's fictional framing. Until the 1960s, censors demanded that criminals be punished before the end of the film. The rise of the Civil Rights movement, the increased use of hallucinogenic drugs, the appeal of free love, and the condemnation of middle-class suburban values provided an opportunity for the revival of the 1930s and 1940s black gangster types. The 1970s black gangsters, however, became saturated with black consciousness, as was apparent in the street heroes Sweetback and Priest (in *Superfly*). The American film industry welcomed black gangster films just as the American music industry would later welcome black gangsta rappers because both forms of entertainment seemed to channel raw black anger and frustration into a marketable enterprise that attracted paying customers regardless of race. Post-1960s black gangster-film heroes and heroines provided their public with profane and sacred fantasies permitted by revised censorship laws and social taboos and still limited certain portrayals of criminality and violence. Most important for the black action film and its depiction of crime and violence was the 1960s Black Power and

Black Arts movements, which introduced new constructions of black heroism and made certain themes more appealing to black action-film audiences.

Francis Ford Coppola's *The Godfather* (Paramount, 1972) exemplifies a system of "law and order" generated by ethnic and racial factors, pitting Italians against Anglo-Americans. Similarly, *The Black Godfather*, a black-oriented remake, pits African American hoods against Italian mafiosi. Both of these films dramatize codes of criminal behavior in an honorable light, but they differ in their ethnic and racial allegiances. Considering the codes of honor depicted in the two films, "law and order" is not a static idea. The established codes reflect a particular audience's perception of "law and order" during a particular time. Classical gangster-film conventions demand that "good guys" be authenticated by city, state, and federal agencies. Taken together, these agents of state authority reflect a more effective consensus and override any particular gangland family.

Sociologically speaking, gangsters are constructed within an imagined but very urban experience that occasions both moral and immoral actions. Studios, screenwriters, directors, film technicians, the sociocultural environment, and the psychological needs of the target audience produce gangster films. Because the black audience has different psychological demands and expressive traditions, gangster films made for blacks are markedly different from white-cast, studio-produced gangster films. The presence of organized and well-dressed black criminals with impeccable speech, the appearance of black police officers and private detectives, the images of black middle-class professionals, and the spiritual striving of poor but proud blacks were rarely present in mainstream Hollywood films of the 1960s and 1970s.

Black gangster films imaginatively reflect the cultural beliefs and social experiences of the black audience during a particular time and place. From the 1960s through the 1970s, black gangster films borrowed some elements from mainstream gangster fare and commonly suggested a conventional understanding of "law and order." Nonetheless, they presented African American concerns, employed African American vaudeville humor, and featured black music. These Afrocentric elements continue to distinguish black-cast from white-cast gangster films, even though major studios produce both types.

GANGSTERS, RAPPERS, AND
BLACK MASCULINITY

In John Singleton's *Boyz N the Hood*, there are educational opportunities that help one to avoid the overdetermined social factors of racism and poverty. Yet some films portray the black urban gangster as a type of "bad nigger." Such films as Mario Van Peebles's *New Jack City* and Ernest Dickerson's *Juice* present the "bad nigger" type as a gangster who preys on members of the black community. If there existed a truly black essential self, would the black gangster's heroic code produce a "bad nigger" driven by unrestrained capitalist desires? The analysis of black gangster films must transcend the narrative limitations of Manichaean constructions of "good" and "bad" blacks and describe the social construction and ideological function of particular types of black gangsters.

Unfortunately, many films simulate essentialist racial notions about black styles and white styles. These films inadvertently create the "bad nigger" as the only appropriate outlet for a community that has limited

An African American father sets his black son on the straight-and-narrow path out of a violent Los Angeles neighborhood: Laurence Fishburne as Jason "Furious" Styles in John Singleton's *Boyz N the Hood* (1991). (Columbia / The Kobal Collection)

socioeconomic resources and opportunities. Thus the narrative explains that blacks should naturally adopt a criminal pose and resist the alleged "assimilated" style of the black middle class. Nonetheless, black folk culture provides examples of transgressive and liberating acts by folk heroes such as Brer Rabbit and Shine. Compromise does not always lead to assimilation.

As *Souls of Sin* evokes a social-realist style, two more recent black gangster films attempt to portray a social-realist style for young black inner-city men caught in the claws of poverty and despair. *Juice* and *Boyz N the Hood* present a complex array of black gangster styles that includes some elements of familial concern and community responsibility. The films work against the too easy equation of black middle-class style with the suppression of the essential "bad nigger" subject and vice versa. Both films present violence, drug addiction, and unwed mothers, but both also resist portraying gangster life and racial assimilation as the two available forms of escape for inner-city dwellers. The gangsta rapper is the post-Negritude muse who entertains the grandchildren of Norman Mailer's white Negroes now facing early retirement.[12] There exist legitimate ideological concerns in the recent black gangster characterizations as performed by rapper Tupac Shakur in his cinematic debut in *Juice*. This is equally true for Tupac Shakur's hyperreal life experience; Tupac allegedly raped a woman in his Manhattan hotel room and was in a gun battle with two Atlanta police officers. Why do critics and his middle-class audience only see the primitive rage of Shakur, whose mother, Assata Shakur, was a member of the Black Panther Party during the 1960s? Shakur's screen portrayals of Bishop in *Juice* and Lucky in Singleton's *Poetic Justice* (Columbia Pictures, 1993) mirror the contained and inarticulate predicament of the protagonist in Eugene O'Neill's *The Hairy Ape*. Social critics ignore the source of his frustrations and anger. He, Tupac Shakur, and those who identify with him are unable to identify with the televised images that reek of economic prosperity. These images claw at inner-city youths who lack educational opportunities that would provide them with jobs, money, and the veneer of middle-class respectability. When the music industry executives finance the "bad nigger" press, it helps to support racist patriarchal myths that are marketable. In the black community, these myths often register the "masculine" zero degree of one's blackness. The bad-boy image of Shakur and other gangsta rappers expresses a raging hatred for white racism, while the image placates the misogynist desires of young white teenagers slumming in blackface. One critic calls it "The Rapper's New Rage."[13] This journalist thereby assists a music industry that makes a rapper black to simulate danger and then displaces gangsta rappers whose words express a politically dangerous plan.

The iconography of many of the black Hollywood films of the 1970s through the 1990s follows the traditions of various action-film genres. Thus *Superfly* and *New Jack City*, two films dealing with black drug dealers and cops, include scenes of criminality, abundant sexuality, and black-on-black violence. *New Jack City*, however, includes an African American, Asian American, and Anglo-American detective team that goes after a very dark-complexioned drug dealer. The light-complexioned black detective beats the dark-skinned dealer senseless. True, the story line provides reasons for this particular intraracial vengeance. Still, the light-complexioned black detective's violence is just another form of police brutality. In *Boyz N the Hood*, the self-hating black policeman is shown for what he is—a killer cop—and the film does not attempt to

An inner-city tale of romance between a hairstylist-poet who has lost her boyfriend to gang violence and a mail carrier whose philosophy of anti-violence kindles a romance: Tupac Shakur as Lucky and Janet Jackson as Justice in John Singleton's *Poetic Justice* (1993). (Columbia / The Kobal Collection)

disguise this hateful violence by demonizing black drug dealers and gang members. What does jailing dealers accomplish if one does not consider that street dealers are merely small players in a larger drama?

In 1998, Milton Friedman observed: "In 1970, 200,000 people were in prison. Today, 1.6 million people are. . . . The attempt to prohibit drugs is by far the major source of the horrendous growth in the prison population."[14] Friedman quoted Sher Hosonka, a former director of Connecticut's addiction services, as saying that in 1995 the United States imprisoned "3,109 black men for every 100,000 of them in the population." Hosonka compares the U.S. incarceration of black men to South Africa's pre-Mandela rate of 729 black men for every 100,000. In discussing the black dealer–white client relationship, Friedman adds that "most customers do not live in the inner cities, most sellers do."

Audiences who view frequent drug dealing in black action films and other popular entertainment forms rarely see a dramatization of this black dealer–white client reality. Most film and literary genres present exotic images of the black inner cities. Black folks on coke are interesting if you view them at a safe suburban distance. Dirty cops, drug cartels, and the effects of incarcerating excessive numbers of young black and Latino men are rarely dramatized. Scenes that portray white drug addicts entering black and Latino communities are left on the cutting-room floor. These cinematic nightmares rarely warrant analysis or documentation. Consequently, it is a gross distortion when film critics and scholars, of whatever political and racial stripe, refer to black action films as "blaxploitation." The black action films that dramatize black dealers are more representative of white exploitation, because such films exhibit a type of Hays Code against interracial drug intimacy.

During the 1990s, African American men and their white male counterparts directed and wrote several black action films. In the 1970s, such action films as Gordon Parks's *Shaft*, Gordon Parks Jr.'s *Superfly*, and Jack Hill's two Pam Grier vehicles *Coffy* (American International, 1973) and *Foxy Brown* (American International, 1974) were widely referred to as blaxploitation films. It is interesting to note that Quentin Tarantino's use of Pam Grier in *Jackie Brown* (Miramax, 1997) pays homage to Grier, her films *Coffy* and *Foxy Brown*, and their white director–writer Jack Hill. And, more than twenty years later, Tarantino wrote an action-film script that features Grier as an intelligent and sexy black heroine.[15]

With more than twenty years' hindsight, it is clear that these types of action films still incorporate a variety of plots and use different film styles. The breadth of black action films made in the independent and

A black western that pairs two African American matinee idols: Harry Belafonte as The Preacher and Sidney Poitier as Buck in Sidney Poitier's directorial debut, *Buck and the Preacher* (1972). (Columbia / The Kobal Collection)

Hollywood film sectors indicates the continued popularity of this genre. Indeed, the genre has outgrown the term *blaxploitation* because it does not exploit blacks and never has. Black action films now include inner-city youth films, gangster films, heist films, and a group of films whose plots and iconography borrow heavily from film genres that were popular during the 1950s and 1960s. This last group of black films includes Mario Van Peebles's black western *Posse* (Polygram, 1993), which continues an earlier tradition of black westerns. For instance, Sidney Poitier's black western *Buck and the Preacher* (Columbia Pictures, 1972) and Gordon Parks Jr.'s *Thomasine and Bushrod* (Columbia Pictures, 1974) present blacks in western settings. As early as the 1930s there existed black westerns, such as the white-directed, black-scripted *Bronze Buckaroo* (Hollywood Productions, 1938), *Harlem on the Prairie* (Associated Pictures, 1939), and *Harlem Rides the Range* (Hollywood Productions, 1939). All three of these independent films feature the black cowboy–singer Herb Jeffries. The black western might appear to be an anomaly to many viewers, but these westerns are most often based on African American experiences as cowboys, buffalo soldiers, and blacks—men and women—who migrated to the West before, during, and after the Civil War.[16]

Further study of black action films that feature cowboys, gangsters, and police agents might consider the function of violence. Is it an act of retribution or is it left unjustified? What is reprehensible about the protagonist's or antagonist's achievement of his or her aspirations? How does the central conflict engage established conventions? Why might one audience permit violence while another audience is appalled by such acts? The answers to these questions provide the black action genre with its psychological relationship to African American spectators at a particular moment in film history.

NOTES

1. For more discussion on the media coverage of Rodney King, Reginald Denny, Anita Hill, Clarence Thomas, and O. J. Simpson, see Mark A. Reid, *Post-Negritude Visual and Literary Culture* (Albany: State University of New York Press, 1997).

2. Here I am suggesting that popular writing on black film expresses the false notion that it started in the 1970s with the boom in black action films such as *Sweet Sweetback*, *Shaft*, and *Superfly*. As recent books on black films and black filmmakers are widely published and black film courses are taught throughout the country, it becomes much harder for scholars, publishers, and audiences to accept this type of uninformed writing on black film.

3. Thomas Cripps, *Slow Fade to Black* (New York: Oxford University Press, 1977), 196.

4. Cripps, *Slow Fade to Black*, 328. In commenting on the significance of *Dark Manhattan*, Cripps notes that the film was "the first from Hollywood." Also see Henry T. Sampson, *Blacks in Black and White: A Source Book on Black Films* (Metuchen, NJ: Scarecrow, 1977), 204.

5. Sampson, *Blacks in Black and White*, 63.

6. Sampson, *Blacks in Black and White*, 63.

7. Sampson, *Blacks in Black and White*, 67.

8. Sampson, *Blacks in Black and White*, 241.

9. G. Williams Jones, *Black Cinema Treasures: Lost and Found* (Denton, TX: University of North Texas Press, 1991), 37.

10. Doris E. Abramson, *Negro Playwrights in the American Theatre, 1925–1959* (New York: Columbia University Press, 1969), 92.

11. Irangate, according to the *tiscali.reference* encyclopedia, was a "US political scandal in 1987 involving senior members of the Reagan administration (the name

echoes the Nixon administration's Watergate). Congressional hearings in 1986–87 revealed that the US government had secretly sold weapons to Iran in 1985 and traded them for hostages held in Lebanon by pro-Iranian militias, and used the profits to supply right-wing Contra guerrillas in Nicaragua with arms. The attempt to get around the law (Boland amendment) specifically prohibiting military assistance to the Contras also broke other laws in the process." "Irangate," *tiscali.reference*, at www .tiscali.co.uk/reference/encyclopaedia/hutchinson/m0020627.html (accessed 18 May 2004).

12. Again, the term *postNegritude* describes the fluidity that reigns in contemporary African and African Diaspora communities. This fluidity challenges conventional beliefs and singular black identity formations. PostNegritude embraces a multitude of struggles without making any one struggle the most important.

13. Malcolm Gladwell, "The Rapper's New Rage," *Washington Post*, 17 December 1992, C1–2.

14. Milton Friedman, "There's No Justice in the War on Drugs," *New York Times*, 1 November 1998, Op-Ed, 19.

15. For a French critic's interesting analysis of black action film and Quentin Tarantino's confessed love of 1970s black film culture, see Samuel Blumenfeld, "Blaxploitation, le cinéma du ghetto," *Le Monde*, 31 March 1998, 28.

16. For more insight into the neglected history of African American life in the West, see Philip Durham and Everett L. Jones, *The Negro Cowboys* (New York: Dodd, Mead, 1965); Lynda Fae Dickson, "The Early Club Movement among Black Women in Denver, 1890–1925," Ph.D. diss., University of Colorado, 1982; Donald A. Grinde Jr. and Quintard Taylor, "Red v. Black: Conflict and Accommodation in the Post–Civil War Indian Territory, 1865–1907," *American Indian Quarterly* 8 (1984): 211–25; Rudolph Lapp, *Blacks in the Gold Rush* (New Haven: Yale University Press, 1977); Kenneth W. Porter, "Negro Labor in the Western Cattle Industry, 1866–1900," *Labor History* 10 (1969): 346–64, 366–68, 370–74; and Arthur L. Tolson, *The Black Oklahomans: A History, 1541–1972* (New Orleans: Edwards Print Co., 1972).

·4·

Two African American Horror Films

$\mathcal{N}$ow let's turn to a comparative analysis of two 1990s black-directed, black-cast horror films. This analysis traces the historical borrowings and representative nature of black-cast films that display horrorlike cinematic elements. Thus this chapter does not discuss horror films that feature racially integrated casts that are primarily composed of nonblack characters. Such films include George A. Romero's *Night of the Living Dead* (Image Ten, 1968), *Dawn of the Dead* (United Film, 1979), and *Day of the Dead* (United Film, 1985); Richard Wenk's *Vamp* (New World Pictures, 1986); Alan Parker's *Angel Heart* (TriStar Pictures, 1987); Wes Craven's *The Serpent and the Rainbow* (Universal Pictures, 1988); and Bernard Rose and Anthony B. Richmond's *Candyman* (TriStar Pictures, 1992). Still, these films are important to consider when discussing the overall history of black representation in the American horror film.

As in the previous chapters, this section maintains a womanist, post-Negritude approach that views race, gender, and sexuality as fluid rather than fixed, as socially constructed rather than biological features. Correspondingly, the analysis is sensitive to the social construction of difference. When analyzing the black horror-film genre, since this genre permits full fantasy, it is important to indicate when difference demonizes characters and creates or resists static notions of good and evil.

Black-directed or black-written horror films with all-black casts were in existence before World War II. For example, Spencer Williams, an African American, wrote and starred in Richard C. Kahn's *Son of Ingagi* (Sack, 1940), which is possibly the first black-cast, horror sound film. The film features a Dr. Frankenstein–like black female scientist who creates a monster that will later kill her. A year after the making of *Son of Ingagi*, Williams directed, produced, and wrote *The Blood of Jesus* (Sack,

1941), a black-cast, religious rural gothic film. *The Blood of Jesus* tells the story of the accidental shooting death of Martha Jackson by her husband Ralph. While Martha lies on her bed between death and life, her spirit is taken on a surrealistic, out-of-body journey in which an African American devil tempts her, but Martha chooses to hold fast to her Christian principles. In 1944, Spencer Williams directed *Go Down, Death* (Sack, 1944), another religious Southern gothic film that featured horrific scenes similar to those found in the classical horror films of the period. Richard C. Kahn's direction of *Son of Ingagi* influenced how Williams would later visually construct his Sack Amusement films. Still, the surrealistic elements found in Williams's films have an undeniable African American religious element that is culturally located in black oratorical style, its emphatic written expression, and its use of religious imagery to conceptualize Hell, Purgatory, and devilish characters who lead innocent souls (Southern, rural blacks) into moral temptation. These elements have surely influenced recent African American horror films.

Yet before the Sack film company produced Spencer Williams's and Richard C. Kahn's 1940s films, Oscar Micheaux's sensual and fleshy *Temptation* (1935) presented carnal desires as morally corrupting and psychologically debilitating. Micheaux's narratives relied on social realism and rarely introduced supernatural elements. In contrast, Williams explores the psychological through fantastic, gothic religious imagery. His religious films evoke a surreal black cultural space in which a soul-thirsty black devil reigns. Micheaux with his licentious images and Williams in his use of Southern black religious imagery together established a rich Afrocentric cultural aesthetic for the black horror-film genre.

During the early 1970s, black-cast horror films were mostly set in the urban North. Bill Gunn's *Ganja and Hess* (Kelly and Jordan, 1973) is a rare example of a 1970s black-cast horror film that African Americans directed, wrote, and produced. However, like most 1970s black-oriented movie fare, mini-major studios distributed white-directed and white-written, black-oriented horror films. Most of these films borrowed heavily from films such as *Dracula* and *Frankenstein*. American International's black-oriented thrillers include William Crain's *Blacula* (1972) and its sequel *Scream, Blacula, Scream!* (1973), William Girdler's *Abby* (1974), and Paul Maslansky's *Sugar Hill* (1974). Other 1970s white-directed, black horror films include William A. Levy's *Blackenstein* (Exclusive Interna-

surreal, dreamlike sequences that organize the forces of
combat urban evil.

ramatic exchange is set in K's New York City apartment,
where the two reminisce about K's Southern past and his
nce in what Joel describes as a sinful city. The dialogue
d Joel recalls the dualistic moral vision found in post–
frican American literature and film. In much of this type
k, the recently migrated black Southerner is a morally sta-
while the black Northern counterpart has somehow
moral nature. This regional moralistic dualism is fore-
n K takes Joel to the neighborhood bar. The bar has an
an clientele that gathers seated at the bar—men alone and
panied by their male companions. The striking exception
male arrangement is one unaccompanied African Ameri-
ose name, quite fittingly, is Temptation (Cynthia Bond).
e, unaccompanied female seated at the bar, Temptation
par protocol only if she is not an item for sexual hire.
ot for sale, and is thus a threat to the would-be guardians
. Bonnie Zimmerman writes, "Women must be forced
nto *normal* womanhood, since left to their own designs,
s easily attracted to a *perverse* form of sexuality, whether
bolical (possession by the devil), or lesbian."[4] As the film
tation encounters K in the bar. Their one–night platonic
nited to a booth in the bar. Her accompanied-by-male
mptation's "normalcy." However, the film reveals K to
d performer—he is an actor by trade. K becomes infatu-
hat he is, believes that Temptation shares his feelings.
that Joel, his sexually inexperienced friend, has met
o is more interested in Joel. K fears that Temptation will
his deep religious convictions and that, as a result, Joel
ludes K.

ent anxiety and self-absorption, K is more reflective of
erican literary trope of the unrefined Southern Christian
nters a sophisticated black temptress and becomes tem-
. It is K, not Joel, who reminds us of the character Zeke
Hallelujah! (MGM, 1929). In this film, Zeke (Daniel
farmer steeped in religion, leaves the farm to sell the
crop in a city. The city is located on a port that is alive
ting gamblers and where he meets a black temptress

tional, 1973) and Crain's *Dr. Black and Mr. Hyde* (Dimension Pictures, 1976).

This process of production and consumption of black horror films describes an overly determined mode of mass-marketed, black-oriented entertainment. It is a colonized mode of production in which there are still undetermined moments when free zones and empty spaces are occupied by radicalized ways of producing, distributing, exhibiting, and viewing black culture on a global screen or television. One need only recall such filmmakers as Oscar Micheaux, Spencer Williams, Safi Faye, Ousmane Sembene, Marlon Riggs, Euzhan Palcy, Julie Dash, Haile Gerima, St. Claire Bourne, Fanta Nacro, Kasi Lemmons, and the many black filmmaking Others.

I want to discuss what is possible and what was done in the 1990s, when "to be young, gifted, and black" meant (and the phrase still brings this forth) contradicting and fragmenting experiences that I call post-

Hollywood's answer to the Black Power era is a black spin on the traditional vampire tale: William Marshall as Mamuwalde/Blacula, an African prince bitten by Dracula, in William Crain's *Blacula* (1972). (The Kobal Collection)

Negritude moments in which there exist radical opportunities to resist self-destructive psychosocial and economic deterministic forces. Still, when these moments surface, there are no guarantees that people will seize the opportunity.

Def by Temptation (Troma Films, 1990) is an independently produced, black horror film whose narrative focus is young, upwardly mobile, black urban professionals. The narrative time is now. AIDS is still a present danger to sexually active, upwardly mobile, black urban professionals—women and men. Upwardly mobile African American women have been constructed as threats—have we forgotten Anita Hill on the right and Lani Guinier on the left? These black women were too right or left in their political affiliations for the centrist politics of Bill Clinton's administration. A balanced understanding of the demonization of black professional women would force the inclusion of Condoleezza Rice into the postNegritude mix of contemporary funk. "When Sue Wears Red," some men want to sing the blues: "And the beauty of Susanna Jones in red, burns in my heart a love-fire sharp like pain."[1]

WHEN SUE WEARS RED, OR TEMPTATION'S DEF JAM

James Bond III directed, wrote, produced, and appeared in *Def by Temptation*. He is best known for his leading roles in Public Broadcasting System screen adaptations of such African American literary classics as *The Sky Is Gray* (1980), *Booker* (1984), and *Go Tell It on the Mountain* (1985). He also appears in the role of a fraternity brother in Spike Lee's *School Daze* (Columbia Pictures, 1988). Ernest Dickerson was the cinematographer for *Def* but left before the film's shooting was completed. *Def*'s executive producers include Nelson George, Kevin Harewood, and Charles Huggins. Paul Laurence scored the original music, and Darnell Martin was the second assistant camera. Martin later directed and wrote *I Like It Like That* (Columbia Pictures, 1994) and *Prison Song* (New Line Cinema, 2001). The film's domestic box-office gross was $2,218,579, which is not so modest for an independent film that received very limited distribution.

Def was shot on location in the Bedford-Stuyvesant and Fort Greene sections of Brooklyn. Bedford-Stuyvesant and Fort Greene are the setting for many of Spike Lee's New York City films. Both neighbor-

hoods held increased popular app
artists and intellectuals took up r
city's cultural and intellectual life
ing the Harlem Renaissance and
Harlem and Manhattan.

The critical reception of *l
international film festival held a
the Best Fantasy Film Award i
Richard Harrington, a *Washingt*

> *Def* is not a masterwork, bi
> director-in-progress. It's bo
> is black, as are most of the c
> brothers did in *House Party*
> taken a tired genre and ma
> stantial exposure to some
> and behind the camera, pe
> white film establishment.[3]

In 1990, it was still impor
the horror film *Def* had an al
American production crew, c
black-directed horror films wi

James Bond's *Def by Tem*
ror-film genre address issues cc
ied in Temptation, a succubus
presents gendered and sexuali
demonizes Temptation's activ
indirectly shows how severa
female demon they create on
sions in a neighborhood bar,
black man who is passionatel
and, as their sexual intercour
end, kills him.

Def features Joel (James
training who travels to New
(Kadeem Hardison), a profes
ferent places, with intermit
Joel's grandmother (Minnie C

son) appea
biblical goc

The fi
a private sp
Northern p
between K
World War
of postwar
ble charact
acquired an
grounded w
African Am
women acc
to this male
can woman

As a si
deviates fro
Temptation
of bar etiqu
into marriag
they might l
extramarital,
develops, Te
encounter is
status secures
be a self-abso
ated and, ma
Later, he lea
Temptation,
make Joel for
will have wh

In his p
the African A
male who en
porarily undo
in King Vido
Haynes), a ru
family's cotto
with crap-sh

named Chick (Nina Mae McKinney). Chick is a fast-talking, cosmopoli-
tan black woman with moves that take Zeke for a hellish ride. Psychologically, Temptation takes K for a similar ride. Fortunately for K, he does
not end up like those men who experience Temptation's bed.

Def reveals, through several episodic, blood-splattering, and murderous sexual encounters, that Temptation is the murderer of many of
the bar's male clients, including the self-indulgent Bartender #1 (John
Canada Terrell). According to patriarchal moral codes, she is unaccompanied and therefore dangerous. She is also dangerous when accompanied,
because, like the black widow, she kills her men, married and otherwise.
She maintains a goddess-like lair, where men are seduced, bedded, and
then bled. The narrative too easily compels a masculinist reading of
Temptation as a vampire who draws from the lifeblood of society. Thus,
Def's primordial monster is Temptation and not those who desire her.
What gods will deliver us from Temptation? We create the feared Other
and then must ostracize this reflection of our repressed selves and
police it.

There still remains, at least for this viewer, an uncomfortable and
interesting moral ambiguity: who preys upon whom? In *Def*, the men
are guiltless when they seek carnal pleasure from Temptation. They are
comforted by their ignorance of her. The men who follow her to bed
believe that their Temptation is a defenseless, sexual object who waits,
with open legs, for every male pursuer. Temptation's carnage is a threat
to important societal norms and beliefs. If a free zone of postNegritude
funk views Temptation as not marked by any fixed notion of gender, she
is a devilish, unmarried, unaccompanied genderless subject who destroys
the harmony of the hegemonic married couple, regardless of the sexuality of that couple.

Dougy (Bill Nunn), one of the men who frequent the bar, occupies
a voyeuristic presence in the background. Unlike the other men, he
never approaches Temptation. Is Dougy a homosexual awaiting the same
male prey as Temptation? The film avoids such an aberrant reading,
which is more threatening to patriarchal order than Temptation's active
sexuality. Dougy tells K that he is investigating the whereabouts of several black men who left the bar with Temptation, but who are now miss-
ing. Dougy is the key for the ideal viewer-reader position. Neither lust
nor vengeance motivates his actions. Nonetheless, his search and its con-
clusions do reestablish patriarchal norms.

Ed Lowry and Richard deCordova describe how the classical film narrative constructs the spectatorial position of an ideal viewer: "The classical film is at least partially defined by a model in which desires embodied in the characters are, in some way, linked to (or conversely, distinguished from) the desires of the 'ideal viewer,' whom the text attempts to center by means of certain conventional techniques."[5]

The audience-viewing position (its moral point of view) for this horror film denies Dougy the "ideal viewer" position. Temptation, Dougy, and the Southern characters Minister Garth, Grandma, and Joel all share the ideal viewer position. The spectator resists or, at the very least, questions the established moral sensibilities, and accordingly, "the viewer's desires may be aligned with the excessive, monstrous desires of the 'mad' character, even as they are tempered by a dependence on the narrative, filmic, legal, and cosmic systems to restrict and punish those desires."[6] This "tempered" disruption permits "mad" pleasure and allows the existence of dialogism between Temptation, her victims, and her ever-so-righteous murderers. *Def* offers several possible readings, and some resist its dominant narrative celebrating patriarchal singular truths. Consequently, K, who fears the worst for his boyhood friend Joel, asks Dougy to help kill Temptation. In a series of crosscut scenes between the Southern-based images of Minister Garth and Grandma and the bar's Northern interior setting, Dougy and K successfully secure patriarchal order by killing Temptation. Together, they perform a ritualistic exorcism of the devil in Miss Jones, Miss Susanna Jones, and a significant part of our unacknowledged humanity.

In the 1990s, there was a resurgence of interest in the black action films of the 1970s, and a new group of African American horror films appeared, notably *Def* and Wes Craven's *Vampire in Brooklyn* (Paramount, 1995), an Eddie Murphy vehicle that Murphy cowrote and coproduced. The new millennium brought Ernest Dickerson's *Bones* (New Line Cinema, 2001). All of these films focus on the African American community and feature a predominantly black cast. I now turn to a discussion of *Bones*, a major studio–produced, African American–directed, and Anglo-American–written black horror film that introduces an inventive interracial mix.

DEM BONES ARE GONNA RISE AGAIN: A MORAL STORY

Ernest Dickerson directed *Bones*, which was scripted by Adam Simon and Tim Metcalfe. Flavio Martinez Labiano provided the cinematography for this Rupert Harvey and Peter Heller production of a New Line film. Elia Cmiral scored the original music for the film, which also included songs by Snoop Dogg and Dr. Dre. The film was shot on location between 1 March and May of 2000 in Vancouver, British Columbia. *Bones* opened on 28 October 2001 in 847 U.S. theaters and grossed $2.82 million the first weekend.[7] These are very small figures for opening theaters and weekend domestic grosses compared to similar black-directed films. For instance, Ernest Dickerson's *Juice* (1992) opened on 1,089 screens and grossed $11.01 million during its first weekend. Dickerson's *Demon Knight* (Universal Pictures, 1995) opened on 1,729 screens and grossed $13.02 million during its first weekend. John Singleton's *Baby Boy* (Columbia Pictures, 2001) took in $8.61 million on 1,533 screens. However, *Bones*'s year-end gross was an enviable $33.46 million; the other three films' year-end receipts were, respectively, $27.42, $27.25, and $28.74 million.[8]

In a series of flashbacks to the 1970s, the film shows Jimmy Bones (Snoop Dogg) as a neighborhood legend revered for his drug-dealing acumen and for safeguarding the welfare of the black community. Because he kept crack out of the black community, a group of friends and adversaries murdered him in a ritualistic communal stabbing that occurred in his mansion. Each of Jimmy's assassins used the same knife to mortally penetrate his chest. One cannot dismiss the homosocial aspect of this ritualistic killing, in particular its covert sadomasochistic homoeroticism. Its biblical references (Christ nailed to the cross, the sword penetrating his side, and the deathly piercing arrows that decorate Saint Sebastian's body) connect the profane imagery to the sacred.

The group stabbing scene portrays an unexpected similarity between Jimmy and such martyrs as Jesus, Saint Sebastian, and the countless black men who were lynched. Racial lynching, however, has a more nefarious and complicated history than can be covered here. Still, racial lynching cannot be separated from its white patriarchal heritage as generated by long-standing racist fears and suppressed desires for the racial Other. In *Def*, black men act out similar patriarchal fears and suppressed carnal desires in their sociosexual relationship with Temptation, the sexual Other.

Patriarchal fears motivate the black men who murder Temptation. Dougy, K, and later Joel correctly suspect that this black woman is a succubus who kills men. Temptation sexually consumes the symbol of patriarchal ordering, the male phallus. A womanist interpretation of

Temptation recognizes her similarity to such Othered women as Joan of Arc, the Salem witches, Harriet Tubman, and Angela Davis. Patriarchal ordering systems viewed these women as threats. In both *Def* and *Bones*, psychosexual anxiety erupts and exposes repressed desires in the form of a dead but living monster. This monster is also an avenging angel whose wrath, with the exception of one white cop, is against black male representatives of repressive and oppressive forces. Black-cast films, regardless of the genre, are insular in their construction of villains, but they also reveal the shared nature of villainy that transcends and transgresses the myth of the black male as noble savage who is immune to the patriarchal desires of his nonblack brothers.

Bones evokes a nostalgic desire for the return of the 1970s, before crack cocaine was distributed in impoverished black neighborhoods.

Because women in *Bones* are without the murderous inclinations of Temptation, they are not the principal targets of male violence. Temptation's violence and the violence directed against her are a sadistic heterosexual exchange. In *Def*, the film's rich, dark color photography exudes a sadomasochistic heterosexual eroticism, which is enhanced by blood-curdling images framed in medium close-up shots and several lengthy sequences of ugly murders. Most of these elements are present in *Bones*, but the erotic quality of *Def* is different.

Bones's male-on-male violence covertly depicts homoerotic sado-masochism. For instance, the film rarely features a chillingly passionate scene when a woman is murdered. Nor is there a sadistically eroticized female lead who comes close to *Def*'s Temptation. On the contrary, the violence in *Bones* explores the hermeneutics of black male violence as anchored in and directed against men by men in a homosocial space— that is, there are usually no women present. This homosocial quality is apparent in the various group shots of the male mobsters who stabbed Jimmy to death, and in Jimmy's ever-so-sanguine revenge against these men. There is a shared pleasure—*jouissance*—in Jimmy's murder and in his meting out of revenge. Jimmy's avenging knife severs the throats of these men, who earlier had used a similar phallus-like object to penetrate his body. The repetition of stabbing and severing heads illustrates the homosocial nexus of same-sex brutal punishment that dominates the imagery in this film. Essentially, the cutting off of heads (phallus) and the penetrating knife blade (erect penis) can be read as a (homo)sexual exchange. This macabre *jouissance* expressed by the phallus-like knife is the tool of choice for the bloody rituals of emasculation in racial lynching.

Jimmy justifiably directs his wrath against the corrupt white cop, Lupovich (Michael T. Weiss); his disloyal mobsters, who include his best friend, Jeremiah Peet (Clifton Powell); and the competing drug lord Eddie Mack (Ricky Harris), who brought crack into the black neighborhood and now controls the neighborhood's drug trade. It is now more than twenty years later; Lupovich has been promoted to detective and monitors the crack trade for a wealthy white politician who finances it and sustains men such as crack kingpin Eddie Mack.

Jeremiah Peet, Jimmy's most trusted friend, who also participated in his murder, has benefited financially from the urban renewal of his former neighborhood. Jeremiah is a respected black community leader and entrepreneur who lives in an upscale, predominantly white neighborhood. He is divorced from his first (black) wife and is now married to a white woman. Jeremiah is the father of Patrick (Khalil Kain) and Bill (Merwin Mondesir) and stepfather of Tia (Katherine Isabelle), the white daughter of his second wife. Tia will adopt the crimson-eyed black dog that is in fact Jimmy Bones.

Patrick, responding to his father's constant retorts about the value of owning property, purchases Jimmy's abandoned mansion. Jeremiah and others murdered Jimmy in this mansion, and his remains lie buried in its basement. Patrick and his brothers and sister are all involved in readying the mansion for its first rave party. During the renovation of the mansion, a disc-jockey friend, Maurice (Sean Amsing), unleashes Jimmy's avenging spirit when he removes Jimmy's signature diamond ring from his skinless finger. In several flashbacks to the 1970s, Jimmy strolls through his neighborhood in Superfly-type attire; the signature ring is shown in close-up shots that connect the diamond ring to its owner. As if opening Pandora's box, Maurice's action rejuvenates Jimmy's skeletal remains and his avenging spirit, and revives the 1970s popular culture that the black action-film genre so excellently documents through the aesthetics of cool, the excess style of its dress, the music, and the film genre's most valued female star—Pam Grier.

Again in *Bones*, the narrative is partially driven by teenagers or young adults. Similar to the previously discussed family films that employ the black youth's point of view, *Bones* presents an interracial group of youths who are siblings or close friends. Their actions and fears provide the moral point of view and balance the murderous and corrupt actions

Two icons of black popular culture are paired as lovers in a revenge thriller that mixes elements of the black action film with the horror thriller: Snoop Dogg as Jimmy Bones and Pam Grier as Pearl in Ernest Dickerson's *Bones* (2001). (New Line / The Kobal Collection / Harvey, Shane)

of the interracial group of adult males—a police officer, a corporate businessman, a community leader, and a group of drug dealers. The target audience for this film is obviously teenage filmgoers.

Pearl (Pam Grier) is Jimmy's widow, a fortune-teller who owns an occult shop within eyeshot of Jimmy's abandoned baroque mansion. Pearl and her daughter by Jimmy, Cynthia (Bianca Lawson), are the only leading characters who still live in the neighborhood Jimmy once controlled. As played by Pam Grier, Pearl is already filled with the essence of black womanist sensuality, which easily overshadows Snoop Dogg's aesthetic of cool, though both actors share a formidable cult following. Pearl's esoteric profession, as with the clairvoyant Mozelle in *Eve's Bayou*, provides her with occult sensibilities that connect her to the surreal underworld of Jimmy Bones. Their erotic scenes are not deathly or spiked with sadomasochism, but they do produce a threatening sense of death. Pearl has a "normalized" sensuality that remains constant by the maternal qualities that protect her daughter and, at rare moments, her knife-wielding, murderous lover. Jimmy takes the form of a black dog—a werewolf—until he has acquired, like Dracula, sufficient energy to morph into Jimmy the man. Pearl lacks any inclination for revenge, but one suspects that she must fear Jimmy's wrath as much as she desires his affections. Toward the end of the film, Pearl, Cynthia, and Patrick, Cynthia's boyfriend, will end Jimmy's second coming. This occurs only after Jimmy takes revenge on all who conspired in his murder.

In one ghostly scene, Jimmy and his daughter Cynthia are strangely presented in a blood-filled bed. The scene alludes to Jimmy's incestuous desire. The scene occurs at night while Cynthia is sleeping. She has a nightmare, and Jimmy's crimson-eyed, black werewolf spirit, the dog in Snoop Dogg, tries to enter his daughter's bed and engage in sex. Because the scene does not conform to the tenets of classical narrative realism, the dream escapes moral strictures against the graphic dramatization of incest and bestiality. Still, and in accordance with Dracula's batty nightly visitations, one can easily take Cynthia's nightmare as evidence of a supernatural sexual ritual. The unfinished nature of his forced incestuous and bestial relationship safely tempers the act, which is also true for interpretations of Cynthia's dream as a wish that appears within the acceptable and pardonable form of a nightmarish dream.

However, in accepting this scene as reflective of Cynthia's repressed Temptation-like desires, one can also view the scene as characteristic of Jimmy's doglike nature. Recall Ed Lowry and Richard deCordova's suggestion that "the viewer's desires may be aligned with the excessive, monstrous desires of the 'mad' character, even as they are tempered by a dependence on the narrative, filmic, legal and cosmic systems to restrict and punish those desires."[9] If this is correct, the safe house of the dream frames Cynthia and the voyeuristic viewer's "mad" desires, which disappear when she is awakened. In contrast, the generic conventions of the horror film frame Cynthia's dream as acceptable narrative fiction.

In an interview, Dickerson said that studio executives told him to cut several scenes that they found morally objectionable. Dickerson intended to shoot the scene with Cynthia (Bianca Lawson) nude in a pool of blood and Jimmy appearing as an apparition. A similar scene appears in Alan Parker's *Angel Heart*, which features Lisa Bonet and Mickey Rourke having sex in a blood-filled bed. In calling to mind this scene, film critic Richard Scheib observes:

> There are some striking set-pieces—a scene where a victim dreams and the walls around him become filled with the tar-covered souls of the undead all reaching out to him; or of Bianca

Lawson's dream of a ghostly figure molesting her under the blankets which turns into a vision of her slowly drowning in a bed of blood—a scene reminiscent of a similar love-making scene in *Angel Heart* (1987); the wonderfully sardonic image of Snoop prowling the streets carrying the still-talking severed heads of his victims. The Alterian Studio creates some striking and novel makeup effects—a *Hellraiser* (directed by Clive Barker, New World Pictures, 1987)-esque fleshly resurrection sequence; bleeding pool tables; a talking dog vomiting up rains of maggots.[10]

In *Bones,* there are also two distinct types of monsters. The living monsters include the upwardly mobile African American man, the corrupt cop, the politician, and the small-time crack dealers. In contrast, Jimmy is a murdered/assassinated neighborhood folk legend. He returns to seek the justice of an eye for an eye. He directs his primitive vengeance at modern urban monsters. Like Temptation, Jimmy is an avenging angel, a vigilante that normalcy will not permit, unless it is in its fictional form, as in this horror film. In *Def,* the primordial monster Temptation threatens patriarchal codes and, like Eve in the Garden, threatens the Tree of Wisdom, which is rooted in normalcy. Those who physically kill Temptation do so to suppress her threats, imagined and real. Jimmy is a similar threat—to the normalized flow of crack cocaine in the black community, all of which is rooted in the basest form of uncontrolled capitalism. Temptation and Jimmy are *abject* characters, the walking dead as avenging angels.

In writing on the horror film and borrowing from Julia Kristeva's *Power of Horror,* Barbara Creed describes the place of the abject, which is similar to the place of Temptation and Jimmy in *Def* and *Bones,* respectively:

> The place of the abject is "the place where meaning collapses, the place where 'I' am not. The abject threatens life; it must be 'radically excluded'" (Kristeva, ibid., 2) from the place of the living subject, propelled away from the body and deposited on the other side of an imaginary border, which separates the self from that which threatens the self. Although the subject must exclude the abject, the abject must, nevertheless, be tolerated for that which threatens to destroy life also helps to define life.[11]

The unfixed polyphony of amorality that reigns in Jimmy and Temptation threatens the moral and peaceful well-being of the world in *Bones* and *Def.* Ironically, the representatives of world order are involved in crack trade in *Bones* and represent oppressive patriarchal norms in *Def.* If the *abject* must be tolerated, as Barbara Creed argues, then Jimmy, Temptation, and the oppressive living forces in both films are unavoidable. The horror film allows us to define life outside of and within a dream that could be destructive as well as liberating.

Let us return to the dream as it ends in the crimson-eyed werewolf's avenging, sexed-up actions that provide Jimmy with destructive and liberating agency. The werewolf's several human kills transform the wolf into Jimmy Bones the man. Maggots and severed heads fill the frame of the final scene as Jimmy returns to the hell that he has temporarily escaped.

Ernest Dickerson's use of previous horror film aesthetics does not begin and end with American studio productions. Dickerson also borrows from the Italian horror film. His international awareness of the horror-film style shows his exposure to a rich international tradition that facilitates his cinematography and choice of narrative strategies. Critics fail when they approach Dickerson's horror films as if they simply arose out of an American horror-film tradition. In an effort to document this transnational sharing between Dickerson and his Italian counterparts, we turn to a brief discussion of his work and that of the master filmmakers of the Italian horror film.

Again, Ernest Dickerson shot the cinematography for *Def*, though he left the production close to its finish. As the director of *Bones*, he hired cinematographer Flavio Martinez Labiano. Ed Gonzalez, film critic for *Slant Magazine*, notes: "Flavio Martinez Labiano's silky blue cinematography owes plenty to [Dario] Argento's stained glass freak shows, deftly bridging gothic present and sepia-toned past (the film's maggot storm is an obvious shot-out to *Suspiria*)."[12] Dickerson confirmed *Bones*'s aesthetic ties to the Italian horror film in interviews included in two documentary films about the making of *Bones*. In Michelle Palmer's documentary shorts *Diggin' Up Bones* (New Line Cinema, 2002) and *Urban Gothic* (New Line Cinema, 2002), Dickerson states that he insisted on a Mario Bava–like visual style. In discussing Anglo-American filmmakers' debt to Italian horror-film directors, David Sanjek mentions Riccardo Freda and Dario Argento and notes: "Of even greater importance and influence is the work of Mario Bava, originally a cinematographer, whose work in the horror genre stretches from 1956 . . . to

1977."[13] Sanjek names several Bava films that made inroads into the development of the *giallo* subgenre:

> More specifically, a number of Bava's films initiated stylistic and thematic trends in the genre: *Black Sunday* (1960) . . . stylishly combined elegant and loathsome imagery while reinvigorating . . . gothic stereotypes; *Blood and Lace* (1964) initiated the "giallo" genre as well as laid the visual and thematic seeds for the slasher film. . . . *Kill Baby Kill* (1966) . . . inverted gothic stereotypes of good and evil by having the power of good embodied by a dark-haired witch while evil is represented by an angelic, blonde young girl.[14]

This Italian horror-film style is also noticeable in George Romero's *Day of the Dead* (1985), a film on which Dickerson was the second unit camera operator.[15] The *giallo* style is also apparent in Dickerson's 1990 cinematographic work on *Def* and in his 2001 direction of *Bones*. Consequently, before he shot *Def* and directed *Bones*, Dickerson was well aware of and gaining greater skill in the narrative and visual elements of the *giallo* horror-film subgenre.[16]

Spike Lee employed Dickerson as his favored cinematographer for such films as *Sarah* (1981), *Joe's Bed-Stuy Barbershop* (1982), *She's Gotta Have It* (Island Pictures, 1986), *School Daze* (Columbia Pictures, 1988), *Do the Right Thing* (Universal Pictures, 1989), *Mo' Better Blues* (Universal Pictures, 1990), *Jungle Fever* (Universal Pictures, 1991), and *Malcolm X* (Warner Brothers, 1992). Critics rarely, if ever, discuss the cinematographic similarities between post-1984 Dickerson-shot films and the classic Italian horror films of Bava and others. Although it is not my aim to discuss this, there does appear to be an undeniable relationship between the cinematography in Italian horror films and Dickerson's color photography. The Italian horror film's cinematographic qualities are prominent visual characteristics of *Def* and *Bones*.

In short, Dickerson's admitted interest in Bava's cinematography is central to the look of both films discussed here. His skilled cinematography and acknowledged respect for the horror films of Mario Bava easily allow one to conclude that, although *Def* and *Bones* reflect African American culture, the films do not spring out of the head of an African Zeus, but are a syncretic blend of several artistic sources, including the Italian Mario Bava and the American George Romero. *Def*'s and *Bones*'s cinematography, eroticism, and gender constructions may retain, resist, and invariably negotiate popular aesthetic trends and genre conventions that compose mainstream horror films.

In summary, *Def* and *Bones* share visual elements with an international horror film genre. Thus, the films transcend any singular national or ethnoracial film identity. Moreover, any reference to these films as African American horror films only indicates that they represent a distinct sociocultural experience, not some essential biological or racial characteristic. Black cinema exists within a historical context that results from social, political, and economic forces.

NOTES

1. Langston Hughes, "When Sue Wears Red," in *Selected Poems of Langston Hughes* (New York: Vintage, 1990), 68.

2. The award went to the much older film *Henry: Portrait of a Serial Killer* (directed by John McNaughton, Fourth World Media, 1986).

3. Richard Harrington, "Def by Temptation," *Washington Post*, 5 June 1990, at www.washingtonpost.com/wp-srv/style/longterm/movies/videos/defbytemptation rharrington_a0aae9.htm (accessed 31 March 2003).

4. Bonnie Zimmerman, "Daughters of Darkness: The Lesbian Vampire on Film," in *Planks of Reason: Essays on the Horror Film*, edited by Barry Keith Grant (Metuchen, NJ: Scarecrow, 1984), 159.

5. Ed Lowry and Richard deCordova, "Enunciation and the Production of Horror in *White Zombie*," in *Planks of Reason*, ed. Barry Keith Grant (Metuchen, NJ: Scarecrow, 1984), 347.

6. Lowry and Cordova, "Enunciation," 348.

7. "*Bones*," *Box Office Prophets* (2001), at www.boxofficeprophets.com/ticker master/oct2001/bones.asp (accessed 30 March 2003).

8. "*Bones*," *Box Office Prophets*.

9. Lowry and deCordova, "Enunciation," 348.

10. Richard Scheib, "*Bones*," *Rotten Tomatoes* (2001), at www.rottentomatoes .com/click/source-973/reviews.php?cats = &letter = d&sortby = movie&page = 12& rid = 314716 (accessed 31 March 2003).

11. Barbara Creed, "Kristeva, Femininity, Abjection," in *The Horror Reader*, ed. E. Ken Gelder (New York: Routledge, 2000), 65. Also see Julia Kristeva, *Powers of Horror: An Essay on Abjection*, trans. Leon S. Roudiez (New York: Columbia University Press, 1982), 2.

12. Ed Gonzalez, "*Bones*," *Slant Magazine* (2001), at www.slantmagazine.com/ film/film_review.asp?ID = 58> (accessed 31 March 2003).

13. David Sanjek, "Fan's Notes: The Horror Film Fanzine," in *The Horror Reader*, ed. E. Ken Gelder (New York: Routledge, 2000), 320.

14. Sanjek, "Fan's Notes," 321.

15. On 10 December 1984, Spike Lee wrote: "Tomorrow afternoon I'm gonna be getting together with Ernest Dickerson. Thursday he's leaving for Florida to shoot second camera on George Romero's *Day of the Dead.*" Spike Lee, *She's Gotta Have It: Inside Guerrilla Filmmaking* (New York: Simon & Schuster, 1987), 112.

16. In "Playing with Genre: An Introduction to the Italian *Giallo*," Gary Needham explains, "One interesting point about the *giallo* in its cinematic form is that it appears to be less fixed as a genre than its written counterpart. The term itself doesn't indicate, as genres often do, an essence, a description or a feeling. It functions in a more peculiar and flexible manner as a conceptual category with highly moveable and permeable boundaries that shift around from year to year to include outright gothic horror (*La lama nel corpo* [*The Murder Clinic*, Emilio Scardimaglia, 1966]), police procedurals (*Milano, morte sospetta di una minorenne* [Sergio Martino, 1975]), crime melodrama (*Così dolce, così perversa* [*So Sweet So Perverse*, Umberto Lenzi, 1969]) and conspiracy films (*Terza ipotesi su un casa di perfetta strategia criminale* [*Who Killed the Prosecutor and Why?*, Giuseppe Vari, 1972]))." Gary Needham, "Playing with Genre: An Introduction to the Italian *Giallo*," in *Fear without Frontiers: Horror Cinema across the Globe*, ed. Steven Jay Schneider (Godalming, England: FAB, 2003), 135.

· 5 ·

Black Female–Centered Film

$\mathscr{H}$ ow do mainstream film narratives assimilate black female protagonists in leading and supporting roles? Analyzing a representative group of black female–centered major motion pictures can help answer this question. As it is an actor's duty to perform her role as best she can, it is not my purpose to equate a role with an actor's moral constitution. Rather, I am interested in the narrative processes that allow and, at other times, restrain certain representations of black womanhood.

The group of films I focus on includes female-centered, black-directed features such as Leslie Harris's rap/hip-hop film *Just Another Girl on the I.R.T* (Miramax, 1993) and F. Gary Gray's black-female heist film *Set It Off* (New Line Cinema, 1996), and such white-directed and white-written films as Richard Pearce's *The Long Walk Home* (Miramax, 1990) and Donald Petrie's *The Associate* (Buena Vista Pictures, 1996). The chapter concludes with a discussion of black-oriented and mainstream films that feature Halle Berry in supporting or leading roles.

BLACK FEMALE LEADS IN
MAJOR MOTION PICTURES

Popular contemporary comedies and melodramas tend to efface the heroine's black sociocultural identity. Comedies such as Ron Shelton's *White Men Can't Jump* (Twentieth Century Fox, 1992) and Richard Benjamin's *Made in America* (Warner Brothers, 1993) comically exaggerate sociocultural differences. Filmgoers watch Gloria Clemente (Rosie Perez) as a streetwise oversexed but lovable Afro-Latina and Sarah Mathews (Whoopi Goldberg) in a romance without a physically inti-

79

mate scene. In *White Men Can't Jump* and *Made in America*, neither the black heroine nor the interracial union is of much dramatic substance. These types of interracial comic romances are no more threatening to the general moviegoer than the pre– and post–World War II cycle of interracial romances that featured white women in blackface. These earlier films include John Stahl's *Imitation of Life* (Universal Pictures, 1934), Elia Kazan's *Pinky* (Twentieth Century Fox, 1949), Delmer Daves's *Kings Go Forth* (United Artists, 1958), Douglas Sirk's *Imitation of Life* (Universal Pictures, 1959), and Hugo Haas's *Night of the Quarter Moon* (Metro-Goldwyn-Mayer, 1959). In one brushstroke, these films paint interracial landscapes in varying racial tones and with another brushstroke hide cultural difference behind the pale mask of white actresses. These blackface romances permitted mainstream film audiences to safely consume the black heroine's corporal image without fear of transgressing codes that forbade miscegenation. Honoring these codes insured the screening of most of these films in the South, where racial segregation laws condemned racial border crossings of all kinds. In many of these films, white blackface actresses—Jeanne Crain as Patricia "Pink" Johnson in *Pinky*, Natalie Wood as Monica Blair in *Kings Go Forth*, and Susan Kohner as Sarah Jane Johnson in Sirk's *Imitation of Life*—gave remarkable performances. Still, employing white actresses to perform roles that black actresses could perform maintains racial discrimination in the studios and keeps black actors performing subservient roles. In the larger community, such practices never offer an alternative that challenges filmgoers to question racist social conventions.

In love, romance, and friendship, the 1990s saw black female film protagonists who were equal in intelligence to their white lovers; and in some films they belonged to the same socioeconomic class. Such films include crime films such as Oliver Franklin's *One False Move* (I.R.S. Media International, 1991) and Carl Franklin's *Devil in a Blue Dress* (TriStar Pictures, 1995). Two noteworthy adolescent interracial romances broke new ground in setting and theme. Anthony Drazan's *Zebrahead* (Columbia Pictures, 1992), set in a black Detroit neighborhood, presents a love affair between a white Jewish boy and a black Christian girl. Both youths attend the same predominantly black high school. The second interracial romance was Maria Maggenti's *The Incredibly True Story of Two Girls in Love* (Fine Line, 1995). This remarkable film explored love between two teenage lesbians, Evie (Nicole Ari Parker) and Randy (Laurel Holloman). Evie is an upper-middle-class black with a boyfriend and Randy is a working-class white living with other lesbians. They attend the same predominantly white high school. In *When Night Is Falling* (October Films, 1995), Canadian filmmaker Patricia Rozema portrays an interracial lesbian romance between two adults. Cheryl Dunye's *The Watermelon Woman* (First Run Features, 1996) presents an interracial lesbian romance plot driven by the debates of the main protagonist (played by Dunye) with her black lesbian friend and her white female lover. *The Watermelon Woman* is considered the first black lesbian–directed feature film; however, there is a much older history of black lesbian filmmaking if we include the short works by Michelle Parkerson, Yvonne Welbon, Cheryl Dunye, and other black women who have made short documentaries and narrative films since the 1980s.

Whoopi Goldberg starred in several films that hinted at interracial heterosexual love. Only a few cast her in a serious romantic relationship. Richard Benjamin's *Made in America* (Warner, 1993), a romantic interracial comedy, awkwardly pairs shop owner Sarah Mathews (Whoopi Goldberg) with car dealership owner Halbert "Hal" Jackson (Ted Danson). She also appeared in Jessie Nelson's *Corrina, Corrina* (New Line Cinema, 1994). In this film, Manny Singer's (Ray Liotta) wife has recently died and left Molly, their preadolescent daughter, in a state of silence. Manny hires Corrina Washington (Whoopi Goldberg) as Molly's nanny. In time, Manny falls in love with Corrina, who has returned Molly to her former talkative self. Whoopi's two romantic interracial unions avoid any graphic display of the carnal pleasure that is found in the independent-produced interracial lesbian films mentioned above, and in most of the heterosexual interracial fare produced by major American studios in the 1990s.

Much too often, black females are cast in supporting roles that recall the black maidservant–confidant to a white client–mistress who has been left without her mate or her previous fame. This is a contemporary reworking of Victor Fleming's *Gone with the Wind* (Metro-Goldwyn-Mayer, 1939) and both the John Stahl and Douglas Sirk versions of *Imitation of Life*. The sentimental melodramatic narrative requires a master–submissive relationship in which the audience and the black servant are completely worried about the psychological health of the white woman. In this narrative form, the black female house servant functions as the object by which the white heroine regains her self-confidence. This is the function of the black protagonists Mammy (Hattie McDaniels) in *Gone with the Wind* and Annie Johnson (Juanita Moore) in Sirk's *Imitation*

A romantic film that presents interracial lesbian love between a black acrobat and a white Christian schoolteacher, the film challenges the conventions of the American romantic comedy film: Rachel Crawford as Petra and Pascale Bussières as Camille in Patricia Rozema's *When Night Is Falling* (1995). (Crucial Pictures / The Kobal Collection / Benjo, Caroline)

The black caretaker-nanny wins the love of her recently widowed white employer and his daughter: Whoopi Goldberg as Corrina Washington, Tina Majorina as Molly Singer, and Ray Liotta as Manny Singer in Jesse Nelson's *Corrina, Corrina* (1994). (New Line / The Kobal Collection)

of Life. They are the spouses-as-confidant to the bachelor–mistress employer. *Gone with the Wind* presents Scarlett O'Hara (Vivien Leigh) depressed over not getting or keeping the man she desires. In Sirk's *Imitation of Life*, Lora Meredith (Lana Turner) is distraught because her successful acting career is on the decline. Regardless of the regional differences between the Southern and Northern settings, the black female performs as the medium–healer for an emotionally unstable white employer.

Two 1990s illustrations of this reworking of the spouse-as-confidant to the bachelor–mistress employer appear in Jerry Zucker's *Ghost* (Paramount, 1990) and John Sayles's *Passion Fish* (Miramax, 1992). In *Ghost*, Oda Mae Brown (Whoopi Goldberg), a pseudopsychic, has this type of *Gone with the Wind* relationship with Molly Jenson (Demi Moore). Oda Mae, like the character Mammy in *Gone with the Wind*, becomes the spiritual medium for Molly to communicate with her recently murdered lover, Sam Wheat (Patrick Swayze). *Passion Fish* also employs a reworked *Imitation of Life* narrative (ironically, this film was written, directed, and independently produced by a politically progressive filmmaker). In *Passion Fish*, Chantelle (Alfre Woodard), a black, reformed drug addict, is nurse–confidant to a depressed May-Alice (Mary McDonnell), a white, bedridden actor who has lost the lead role on a popular televised soap opera. In *Ghost* and *Passion Fish*, the black female protagonists Oda Mae and Chantelle are supporting roles in every sense of the word, since their actions return their white female counterparts, Molly and May-Alice, to a healthy psychological state that provides narrative closure. The altruism of Oda Mae and Chantelle is commendable, but an equivalent exchange by their white peers is not forthcoming. Thus the films present black female protagonists as selfless and establish their goodwill and Christian altruism as the only means by which such black heroines can enter the sentimental hearts and dull minds of a mainstream audience. Such presentations reinforce age-old racist beliefs that black women are carefree and complacent "mammies" with preordained gifts to nurse and comfort white female Others and their children. Contrarily, the constancy of this reworked narrative belittles the filmgoer's ability to accept films that introduce innovative interracial friendships between women and that challenge the spouse-as-confidant to the bachelor–mistress employer paradigm. The black protagonist reaps little beyond pay for her services to the white female lead. This codependent type of interracial female bonding valorizes black self-sacrificing characters and white propensity to freely consume the Other. This is also apparent in interracial romances between black men and white females, as in Todd Haynes's *Far from Heaven* (Focus Films, 2002). Such narratives rarely explore the racial and economic factors that determine the film narrative's construction of these servant–mistress relationships in contemporary cinema and, if we press further, the salary disparity between the black and white female costars. This is not to suggest that this chapter intends such a discussion, but the issue is worth mentioning.

At least two Whoopi Goldberg vehicles introduce interracial female bonding narratives that resist the white woman protagonist's dependence on black female as physical and spiritual caretaker. Major studios produced the films that featured black female protagonists in roles of equal or of more significance and dramatized issues concerning race and gender. In Richard Pearce's *The Long Walk Home* (Miramax, 1990) and *The Associate* (Buena Vista Pictures, 1996), the black female lead promotes feminist and African American concerns. Although such films were few in number, the 1990s brought major studio films that feature images of empowered black female protagonists in romance, marriage, and divorce. The roles present black females who exercise agency over their situation. For instance, Angela Bassett's leading roles in Forest Whitaker's *Waiting to Exhale* (Twentieth Century Fox, 1995), Kathryn Bigelow's *Strange Days* (Twentieth Century Fox, 1995), and Kevin Sullivan's *How Stella Got Her Groove Back* (Twentieth Century Fox, 1998) were exceptions to the general lack of fitting roles for black women in Hollywood. Though rare in number, these films show black female protagonists who are equal in intelligence and socioeconomic status to the white costar or black male costar.

A successful San Francisco stockbroker is persuaded by her New York girlfriend to take a break from her high-pressured job and responsibilities as a single parent: Whoopi Goldberg as Delilah Abraham and Angela Bassett as Stella Payne in Kevin Rodney Sullivan's *How Stella Got Her Groove Back* (1998). (20th Century Fox / The Kobal Collection / Stevens, D)

FROM PASSIVE MARGIN TO ACTION-ORIENTED MAINSTREAM

In the early 1970s, Julie Dash, Alile Sharon Larkin, Haile Gerima, and other black independent filmmakers established cinematic strategies that used female-centered narratives that articulated a black womanist vision. Today, this vision is present in such 1990s films as Leslie Harris's *Just Another Girl on the I.R.T.* (Miramax, 1992) that were produced and distributed by mini-major studios and directed and written by black women. It is also seen in certain male-directed or male-written, major studio productions, such as F. Gary Gray's *Set It Off* (New Line Cinema, 1996), a black female heist film, and Donald Petrie's *The Associate* (Buena Vista Pictures, 1996), a white-directed Whoopi Goldberg vehicle. I turn now to Harris's *Just Another Girl on the I.R.T.* and its representation of teen pregnancy.

The major problem that generates the film's narrative action involves Chantel Mitchell (Ariyan A. Johnson), a pregnant Brooklyn teenager in her last year of high school. She must decide whether to undergo an abortion and attend college without parental responsibilities. Chantel seriously considers reasons why abortion would be the best choice. *Just Another Girl* ends as Chantel accepts her motherhood duties and postpones entering college. The film dramatizes such important contemporary social issues as teenage pregnancy, safe-sex practices, and obstacles that black youths face in continuing their education beyond high school.

Black leaders have often criticized the presence of black-on-black violence and the overabundance of sexual imagery in black films. Regarding the sexual imagery and adolescent pregnancy in this film, these leaders criticized Chantel's devil-may-care attitude and argued that Chantel presents a bad role model for black adolescent girls to follow. However, if one looks beyond the film's mise-en-scène of hip-hop music, urban dress, aggressive language, and swagger, which defines most hip-hop and rap films, the black leaders and taste makers might realize that the film asks its black urban audience, particularly the females, to avoid unwanted pregnancies, practice safe sex, and continue their education, regardless of the obstacles they encounter. *Just Another Girl*, therefore, echoes the call for condom use that was earlier articulated in *House Party* (1990), another black-directed and black-written hip-hop film of the period. In broadening the issues covered in the hip-hop film sub-

One troubled, pregnant, high school girl with hip-hop style and self-determination keeps her eye on the prize—a college education: Ariyan A. Johnson as Chantel Mitchell in Leslie Harris's *Just Another Girl on the I.R.T.* (1992). (Miramax / The Kobal Collection)

genre, *Just Another Girl* introduces a female-centered narrative in which a black adolescent, Chantel, determines sexual activity and childbirth. Neither her black boyfriend nor the legal and moral apparatus of the state have agency over Chantel's body and her decision to keep the baby. The film empowers its lower-class, teenage, unwed mother, who in American news broadcasts is popularly condemned. The centrist politics of Bill Clinton and the conservative values of Ronald Reagan–George Bush–George W. Bush Republicans have demonized black unwed mothers and have held them responsible for the destruction of the (black) American family. Black leaders and social commentators are no better when they ask filmmakers to limit their film depictions of African American life to upbeat, middle-class black characters and their concerns. Such a narrow view of contemporary black life ignores and leaves undeveloped the *Just Another Girl* black heroine. Chantel expresses a degree of ambition, confidence, and determination similar to that of the female protagonists in such gynocentric black independent films as Alile Sharon Larkin's *A Different Image* (1981), Tracy Moffatt's *Nice Coloured Girls* (1987), and Julie Dash's *Daughters of the Dust* (Kino, 1991). Chantel resembles such black teenage heroines in mini-major films written and directed by black women as Eve Batiste (Jurnee Smollett) in Kasi Lemmons's *Eve's Bayou* (Trimark, 1997) and Monica Wright (Sanaa Lathan) in Gina Prince-Blythewood's *Love and Basketball* (New Line Cinema, 2000).

Leslie Harris's *Just Another Girl* reflects the black popular music and clothing styles of the late 1980s and early 1990s. Harris saturates the film with hip-hop music and loose-fitting clothing as worn by her target audience—young black urban adolescents. Certainly, the rap, hip-hop, and urban home-girl/boy clothing style attracts the urban adolescent film audience and those older audience members who are interested in this particular black cultural style. This interest in black contemporary music forms is not new and predates the soul music explosion heralded by the black action films of the 1970s. More than a decade earlier, European filmmakers had hired black jazz composers to write musical scores for their films. Such jazz film scores include Miles Davis's original music score for Louis Malle's *Elevator to the Gallows* (*Ascenseur pour l'échafaud*; Lux, 1958), Thelonius Monk's music score for Roger Vadim's *Dangerous Liaisons* (*Les liaisons dangereuses*; Ariane Distribution, 1959), and Chico Hamilton's music score for Roman Polanski's *Repulsion* (Royal Films International, 1965). In Hollywood, jazz composer Quincy Jones was probably the first African American to score the music for a major studio production. He composed the original music for Sidney Lumet's *The Pawnbroker* (American International Pictures, 1964) and Sydney Pollack's *The Slender Thread* (Paramount, 1965). Thus black composers have a more than fifty-year history of writing the musical scores of important art films and Hollywood studio productions.

Two college basketball players fall in love and struggle to maintain their love as their professional ambitions place obstacles in their paths to possible fame and fortune: Sanaa Lathan as Monica Wright and Omar Epps as Quincy McCall in Gina Prince-Blythewood's *Love and Basketball* (2000). (New Line / The Kobal Collection / Baldwin, Sidney)

F. Gary Gray's *Set It Off* (New Line Cinema, 1996) features a group of four black female friends who organize a series of bank robberies. One member of the female gang is the single, upwardly mobile Frankie (Vivica A. Fox), a bank teller who loses her job after a bank official falsely accuses her of conspiring with a man who robbed the bank. One of the two maternal females is Stony (Jada Pinkett Smith), who after the death of both her parents cares for her teenage brother and encourages him to attend college. Tisean (Kimberly Elise), a single mother, is the other female with maternal characteristics. The fourth member of this exclusively female group is Cleo (Queen Latifah), who exhibits the macho qualities of the quintessential 1970s black action hero. Cleo possesses a fast, expensive car, large-caliber guns, gold jewelry, and clothes that deemphasize her extralarge female physiology and gender. These extrafetishistic accessories—car, guns, jewelry, and Ursula (Samantha MacLachlan), Cleo's passive, svelte female lover—make Cleo *somebody* instead of a black lesbian of nothingness. These fetishized objects set off Cleo's exotic black masculinity of consumption and reduce Ursula to a black Other as sylphlike woman. Maternal responsibilities are not Frankie's concern, since she is a semiprofessional, single woman. Cleo, the girl-boy action hero, honors no conventional moral pretensions, as do the maternal characters Stony and Tisean. In *Set It Off*, Cleo and Ursula offer a lesbian slant to the typical black male as action hero as bank robber. Latifah plays a macho (read stereotyped dyke) bank robber whose girlfriend Ursula is a sexy, nubile black woman. The sexy black girlfriend and the female group of bank robbers remain anonymous but recognizable urban black women. This feminized version of the bank heist film arrives one year after Albert and Allen Hughes's *Dead Presidents* (Buena Vista Pictures, 1995), a film that dramatizes a group of four black men with a similar nihilistic "by any means necessary" death wish for want of money. The Cleo–Ursula lesbian union presents an alternative to the typical heterosexual configuration of male gangster and female moll companion. Together, Cleo, Frankie, Stony, and Tisean form a womanist bank-robbing quartet and provide an unrestrained and inclusive image of female characterization in black action films.

POSTNEGRITUDE READINGS OF BLACK FEMALE LEADS: WHOOPI AND HALLE

Here, I move analysis away from a narrow focus on black-directed films to discuss Whoopi Goldberg and Halle Berry, the two most significant black actresses of the 1990s. Most black celebrities are burdened with the responsibility of representing all African Americans, though their individual experiences may cover a more complex and less hierarchical understanding of race, ethnicity, gender, and sexuality that is more given

An all-girl heist film that features a black lesbian romance and friendship between a lesbian and three heterosexual women: Jada Pinkett-Smith as Lida "Stony" Newsome, Kimberly Elise as Tisean "T.T." Williams, Queen Latifah as Cleopatra "Cleo" Sims, and Vivica A. Fox as Francesca "Frankie" Sutton in F. Gary Gray's *Set It Off* (1996). (New Line / The Kobal Collection)

to a womanist, postNegritude understanding of blackness as fluid and ever changing in historical time and geographical space.

In the case of Whoopi Goldberg, a womanist postNegritude analysis is interested in Whoopi's antagonistic encounters with certain black leaders who are critical of her inventive stand-up comedy work and her black female–centered films. Whoopi's seminal but overlooked performance in Donald Petrie's *The Associate* (Buena Vista Pictures, 1996) explores important career issues that face middle-class African Americans and women as they enter positions that were formerly occupied by middle- and upper-class white males.

Many of the criticisms directed at Whoopi Goldberg's making whoopee unsafely reveal black middle-class anxiety. For instance, one can easily recall the disdain she attracted over Ted Danson's blackface performance at the Friar's Club roast in her honor. Additionally, her interracial affairs with one married and several single white men were irksome to some blacks, who will never forgive her womanist performance and Steven Spielberg's direction of *The Color Purple* (Warner Brothers, 1985). There are still other complaints directed at Whoopi's innumerable film roles as a caretaker or romantic go-between for whites, as discussed earlier in this chapter. The most ridiculous criticisms are those concerning her physical appearance. I cannot recall the source, but these criticisms suggested that her hairstyle and too-colorful, loose-fitting clothes do not best represent a black woman of her wealth and professional stature. Consequently, Whoopi wavers between being a National Association for the Advancement of Colored People (NAACP) Image awardee and, intermittently, a black persona non grata to certain blacks. This dilemma is ripe for an ethnic-based theory of reception.

There is no unified African American audience, nor should there be one. There were many criticisms of Alice Walker's 1982 novel *The Color Purple* and Steven Spielberg's 1985 screen adaptation of this work. There are many instances illustrating the diverse receptions that any given ethnic community might produce. PostNegritude is sensitive to the complex processes of film reception, and this allows a dynamic reading of Whoopi Goldberg's stage and screen performances.[1] Reading Whoopi through a postNegritude lens darkly, one becomes aware of the unsafe and profane elements of Whoopi Goldberg's film performances that challenge monolithic forms of blackness and womanhood.[2] An example of this occurs in Whoopi's performance in Donald Petrie's *The Associate* (Buena Vista Pictures, 1996). *The Associate* is an American remake of René Gainville's French film *L'Associé* (FR3, 1979), which was adapted from the Jenaro Prieto novel *El Socio*. The main protagonist, Laurel Ayres (Whoopi Goldberg), resists submissive forms of blackness and womanhood and questions those characters whose actions marginalize blacks and women who have white-collar professional jobs and those who service them.[3]

In *The Associate*, black Laurel Ayres reverses Ted Danson's real blackface Friar's Club roast performance by appearing in whiteface and male drag before an exclusive group of white executive businessmen. She does so in the person of her fictive white male business partner, Robert S. Cutty. Like the Friar's Club invitational roast that honors mostly white male comedians, the Peabody Club unknowingly invites Robert Cutty to present the annual lecture that is given by the year's most successful business executive. The Peabody Club is an exclusively white male business club that honors the business acumen of Laurel Ayres, whose race and gender must be veiled/masked as white Robert Cutty. Interestingly, the Friar's Club roast and the Peabody Club dinner honor a black woman as a talented screen actor and as a skilled stock market analyst, respectively.

The ballroom where the Peabody Club annual dinner takes place is defined by the socioeconomic architectural barriers that separate both the female secretarial staff and black male waiters who enter the ballroom only to serve its exclusive white male occupants, to whom Laurel Ayres's black and female presence is hidden behind male dress and white face paint. Her black and female peers, when not serving the captains of industry, stand waiting at the ballroom door entrance. The border that separates the space before and beyond the ballroom entrance also separates the men from the boys and girls; Laurel Ayres transgresses because she is black and a woman. When Laurel Ayres, dressed as Robert S. Cutty, kisses Frank (Tim Daly), her former colleague who receives the promotion that Ayres rightfully deserved, she performs an additional transgression of homosexual intimacy. Since she is a well-heeled, honored guest, they ignore the sexual transgression. However, when Laurel Ayres reveals her race and gender, she disrupts the white male status quo.

The film's representation of the highly competitive capital-intensive world of the Peabody Club shocks its audience in its presentation of African men in the space, but only in subservient positions. The invisibility of the black waiters to the wealthy white male guests recalls the cinematic representation of the white plantation owner's attitude toward his black house servants. In the scene, women, a drag queen, and news reporters are likewise marginalized, since they occupy the exterior service space of the black waiters. All observe but do not participate in the games and feasting of big capital. Like most mainstream Hollywood utopian fare, the film instructs and provides an unthreatening closure where those in power agree to accept a modicum of change.

In an exclusively white male corporate world, the financial analyst Laurel Ayres creates spaces for women and blacks. The film indicates how women are typecast as Wall Street secretaries and black males are silent or silenced waiters at exclusive, white Wall Street financial clubs. In this cinematic space, a postNegritude funk rebuffs both Laurel Ayres's white male colleagues and any spectator who feels threatened by Laurel Ayres's not-so-safe performances at the Peabody Club. This is also true for those who felt threatened by the Whoopi Goldberg–Ted Danson comic performance at the Friar's Club roast. Why should Laurel Ayres conform to middle-class pretensions that uphold phallocentric business practices and racist conventions? Admittedly, this film is about making

Whoopi Goldberg in a role that provides a transracial womanist agency and dramatizes class conflicts: Whoopi Goldberg as Laurel Ayres and Dianne Wiest as Sally in
Donald Petrie's *The Associate* (1996). (Polygram / The Kobal Collection)

money for multinationals and the white men who consort in places like
the Peabody Club. Laurel Ayres is a successful black woman whose intelligence and business acumen reward her in a highly competitive, male-
dominated corporate world. This is also true for Whoopi Goldberg in
the American entertainment industry. In describing Whoopi Goldberg's
skill and success as an independent producer, Neal Koch, a *New York
Times* reporter, writes,

> The episode illustrates the independent management style with
> which Ms. Goldberg, 46, has built her entertainment enterprise. It
> also demonstrates that even as increasing corporate consolidations
> crowd independent producers out of Hollywood, a few smart
> players with their own bankrolls and name recognition can still
> find a niche. In contrast to Ms. Goldberg's loud screen personal-
> ity, she has played her role as businesswoman with quiet determi-
> nation.[4]

Chantel Mitchell, the protagonist in *Just Another Girl*, shares a few similarities with Whoopi Goldberg. Whoopi and Chantel both grew up in
New York City's housing projects, never finished high school, and
became parents at a young age. A *New York Times* article reported that
Whoopi Goldberg was born Caryn Johnson in Manhattan's Chelsea
projects in 1955. She is a self-acknowledged former drug addict,
divorced three times, a mother of one daughter, and a grandmother to
three.[5] In 1973, Whoopi, then Caryn Johnson, married Alvin Martin,
her first husband, and gave birth to her only daughter, Alex Martin.
Whoopi was probably in her late teens when she gave birth to Alex.

In *The Order of Things*, Michel Foucault writes, "Modern thought
is advancing toward that region where man's Other must become the
Same as himself."[6] Thus, a Whoopi–Laurel Ayres's postNegritude is that
transitional stage when a significant number of black women question
the belief that blacks should conform as nearly as possible to norms and
standards conceived as immutable and identical for one and all blacks the
world over.[7]

One can apply Houston A. Baker's description of "the deformation
of mastery" to Ted Danson's appearance in blackface at the Friar's Club
roast and Laurel Ayres's whiteface gender-bending performance at the
Peabody Club. The two performances exemplify what Baker calls "the
mastery of form" and "the deformation of mastery." He writes,

> The mastery of form conceals, disguises, floats like a trickster but-
> terfly in order to sting like a bee. The deformation of mastery, by
> contrast, is Morris Day singing "Jungle Love," advertising, with
> certainty, his unabashed badness—which is not always conjoined
> with violence. Deformation is go(uer)rilla action in the face of
> acknowledged adversaries.[8]

The politics of mainstream mediocrity would silence Whoopi's unortho-
dox style of dress and choice of interracial intimacies. Her dress, private
affairs, and entrepreneurial wit are markers of her individual, inventive
creative agency. Frantz Fanon's concept of the "collective unconscious"
precisely describes this as "purely and simply, the sum of prejudices,
myths, collective attitudes of a given group. The collective unconscious
is cultural, which means acquired."[9] Like Laurel Ayres, Whoopi's private
and public performance cannot be limited to conventional notions of
respectability in dress and love. If Laurel Ayres signifies an idea rather

than a mere fictive character in a film narrative, then Ayres is relevant to a postNegritude construction of black identity and culture. Similarly, Whoopi Goldberg, in her professional and public life, is best seen as a fluid dynamic idea of blackness that escapes the dogmatic, dehumanizing, and racist genetic thinking that circulates when nations and their people become anxious for ready-made and constant truths that do not change with time.

Reading against the racial identity grain provides a critical strategy for an alternative reading of Whoopi Goldberg that resists the conventional, respectable forms of black cultural identity. A postNegritude critical reading strategy scrutinizes patriarchal and nationalist discourses that want to remake Whoopi into a safe commodity for international consumption as a few of her film roles—in *Ghost* and *Corrina, Corrina*—do. This brief discussion of *The Associate* indicates the ideological conflicts that arise when black subjects resist patriarchy, racism, and other forms of discrimination. Additionally, it shows how Whoopi, as a talented actor and public figure, dramatizes the contemporary debate over the constitution of black cultural identity when race is no longer (and never truly was) the sole criterion for defining the multitude of black experiences.

The television and motion picture industry, the African American community, and her acting colleagues have recognized the quality of Halle Berry's television and film work. As early as 1995, Berry received the NAACP Image award for Outstanding Lead Actress in a Television Movie or Miniseries for John Erman's *Queen* (CBS, 1993), an Alex Haley teleplay in which she plays the daughter of a black slave woman and the white plantation owner. In 2000, she received the same NAACP Image award for her performance as Dorothy Dandridge in Martha Coolidge's HBO biopic *Introducing Dorothy Dandridge* (HBO, 1999), on which Berry was one of the five executive producers. Several representative entertainment organizations gave her the Screen Actors Guild award for Outstanding Performance by a Female Actor in a Television Movie or Miniseries, an Emmy for Outstanding Lead Actress in a Miniseries or a Movie, and a Golden Globe for Best Performance by an Actress in a Miniseries or Motion Picture Made for TV. In 2001, the National Board of Review awarded Halle Berry the Best Actress award for *Monster's Ball* (Lions Gate Films, 2001). The following year, and for the same performance, Berry received Hollywood's most prestigious acting award, an Oscar for Best Actress in a Leading Role, and best actress awards from the Screen Actors Guild, Black Entertainment Television, and the Berlin International Film Festival.

In 2002 and 2004, respectively, the NAACP once more acknowledged Berry's acting with Image awards for Outstanding Actress in a Motion Picture for *Swordfish* (2001) and *Gothika* (2003), and in 2003 the NAACP gave her the Image award for Outstanding Supporting Actress in a Motion Picture for the James Bond sequel *Die Another Day* (2002).

Halle Berry's major film debut was in Spike Lee's *Jungle Fever* (Universal Pictures, 1991). She played Vivian, the crack-addicted girlfriend of Gator (Samuel L. Jackson), the crack-addicted brother of Flipper (Wesley Snipes). Other black-oriented films in which Berry has played leading roles include two romantic comedies, Kevin Hooks's *Strictly Business* (Warner Brothers, 1991) and Reginald Hudlin's *Boomerang* (Paramount Pictures, 1992). In *Strictly Business*, she appears in the role of Natalie, whom Waymon Tinsdale III (Joseph C. Phillips) pursues. Waymon is the only black executive in a major Manhattan real estate firm. When Waymon pursues Natalie, his travels lead him to Manhattan's black neighborhood. He discovers black urban lower-class life that his Ivy League education and his career had obscured. Waymon's trajectory through the black community in search of Natalie, his black Halle grail, humanizes him and wins him the object of his desire—Natalie.

Eddie Murphy wrote and stars in *Boomerang*, a romantic comedy about black cosmetics company executives. Jacqueline Broyer (Robin Givens), the top executive of the cosmetic firm, seduces the lower-level advertising executive Marcus Graham (Eddie Murphy). For no apparent reason, Jacqueline drops Marcus, then rekindles their affair, only to drop him for a second time. Jacqueline's abuse turns Marcus into a heartbroken but sensitive black man. He has lost his former self-assured, macho posturing and womanizing attitude. Jacqueline's mistreatment functions as a corrective that prepares Marcus for a mutually caring relationship with Jacqueline's executive assistant, Angela Lewis (Halle Berry). Angela is a sensitive black who helps Marcus recover his self-assured attitude and drive—his masculinity.

Many of Halle Berry's most recent roles are in films where she is cast as the sole black in a leading or supporting role, giving her career a trajectory similar to those of black male actors such as Denzel Washington and Cuba Gooding Jr. and black female actors such as Whoopi Goldberg and Angela Bassett. Berry's leading roles in non–black-oriented films include a supporting role in Stephen Gyllenhaal's *Losing Isaiah* (Paramount, 1995). She appears as female lead to white males in films such as Warren Beatty's *Bulworth* (Twentieth Century Fox, 1998), Dominic Sena's *Swordfish* (Warner Brothers, 2001), Marc Forster's *Monster's Ball* (Lions Gate Films, 2001), Lee Tamahori's *Die Another Day* (MGM, 2002), and Mathieu Kassovitz's *Gothika* (Warner Brothers, 2003).

In *Losing Isaiah*, Berry plays Khaila Richards, a reformed drug addict. During a delirious passage when she withdraws from drugs, Richards falls unconscious after placing her infant son Isaiah (Marc John Jefferies) in a container. Garbage men discover the abandoned child and take him to the hospital. Richards awakens from her stupor to discover that Isaiah is gone, and she becomes hysterical and consumed with guilt. Richards hires attorney Kadar Lewis (Samuel L. Jackson) to petition the legal system for the return of her child, whose adoptive parents, Dr. Margaret Lewin and her husband Charles (Jessica Lange and David Strathairn), are a white couple with a teenage daughter.

Bulworth features Nina (Halle Berry), a streetwise South Central Los Angeles young adult who becomes the lover of Sen. Jay Billington Bulworth (Warren Beatty), a married, middle-aged, liberal California Dem-

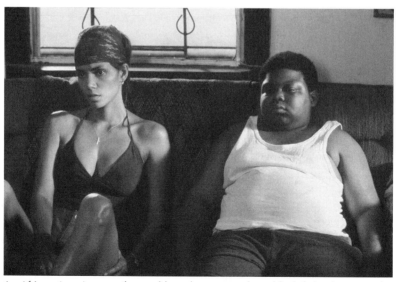

An African American mother and her obese son, whose black father has recently been executed by the State of Georgia: Halle Berry as Leticia and Coronji Calhoun as Tyrell in Mark Forster's *Monster's Ball* (2001). (Lions Gate / The Kobal Collection / Bulliard, Jeanne Louise)

ocrat who is up for reelection in 1996. Jay Bulworth is at a speaking engagement when he meets a group of young black women whom he charms with his radical social program and criticism of the Republican and Democratic Parties. The women follow Jay into his limousine and direct him to a Los Angeles hip-hop club, where they smoke marijuana. Nina, a member of this group, ultimately attracts his eye. Nina and Jay dance the night away and end up at her family's South Central Los Angeles home. Jay spends several days in South Central with Nina. He witnesses young kids selling crack and encounters residents whose children have died in drive-by shootings and its crossfire. Meeting Nina and his stay in South Central Los Angeles revive Jay's radical liberalism. He begins to incorporate rap in his reelection campaign speeches, which discuss social policy programs to improve the lives of the urban poor. Jay had placed a contract on his own life with the Mafia. Now that he is reborn, he seeks to withdraw the contract. Unfortunately, the film suggests a type of blackface remedy for the Democratic Party's turn toward neoconservatism since President Jimmy Carter. The diagnosis requires three types of appropriations and consumptions. The white male Democratic politician must visit the lower-class black constituency; most politicians perform these "town hall" meetings with various groups. Jay's Odysseus-like travels take him further than wise discretion permits any politician, since his infidelity is public and it is with a young, black female. Equally self-destructive for a Republican or Democratic candidate is the promotion of socialism at a predominantly mainstream gathering.

Set in Georgia, *Monster's Ball* features Leticia Musgrove (Halle Berry) and Hank Grotowski (Billy Bob Thornton) as perhaps the most depressing and mismatched interracial couple that Hollywood has ever brought to the screen. For her performance, Berry received an Oscar for Best Actress. She was the first African American woman to win this award, although Dorothy Dandridge was the first black woman nominated in this category. Leticia is black, the divorced wife of Lawrence (Sean Puffy Combs), a death-row inmate, and mother of Tyrell (Coronji Calhoun), an overweight boy. Hank is a white jail guard, a bully of a father to Sonny (Heath Ledger), and son of Buck (Peter Boyle), a rabid racist. Leticia and Hank, though of different races and separated by Georgia's still-honored racial codes, must endure the deaths of their three family members. Hank assists in the state-sanctioned murder of Leticia's former husband and forces Sonny to participate. Sonny does not share

Hank's stoic obedience to the penitentiary job or Buck's racism. In fact, Sonny secretly befriends his black neighbors and their children. He becomes sick and vomits when Hank forces him to participate in Lawrence's execution. Sonny is overburdened with guilt for his father's cruel actions as a penitentiary guard. His grandfather's virulent racism against the children of his black neighbors fills Sonny with shame. In an effort to escape, Sonny kills himself with his service revolver. Buck's response to Sonny's suicide is to say that he was weak. Later, Buck dies from natural causes. The film tends to say that the aging villains will outlive their children who have better moral vision.

Hank reflects on all that has transpired and discovers that he is an empty man. Correspondingly, Leticia loses her former husband to execution and her son when a car fatally hits him. The accident brings Hank, Leticia, and Tyrell together because Hank stops to aid them. Hank places the unconscious and bleeding Tyrell in his car and drives to the hospital while trying to comfort a very hysterical Leticia. The three form a Southern family whose male children, a dead white Sonny and a dying black Tyrell, are sacrificial lambs who permit the film's childless black mother and white father to rewrite their Southern lives. Hank becomes a sensitive person, befriends his black neighbors, and opens his home and bed to Leticia. As reparations for the South's racist past, Hank assumes Leticia's financial burdens and offers shelter against the storm of Southern realities that few blacks escape. They are both lonely and empty. Later, she discovers that he participated in the State of Georgia's execution of her former husband. If Leticia forgives Hank, it will acknowledge that Sonny and Tyrell's deaths awaken an alternative South that resists the continuance of racist conventions and men like Buck. The film does not stress this upbeat reading but rather offers loneliness as the motive for their actions.

In *Bulworth* and *Monster's Ball*, the characters Nina and Leticia are desired sexualized objects whose atavism humanizes their white male lovers. Like *Boomerang*'s Angela, who rejuvenates Marcus's ego and professional drive, *Bulworth*'s Nina and *Monster's Ball*'s Leticia perform a similar function for Jay and Hank, respectively. Berry's roles in the three films operate in a like fashion, since they reestablish the male character's self-esteem. In the pursuit of Natalie, Nina, and Leticia, respectively, Waymon, Jay, and Hank observe the socioeconomic realities of the nearby black community. In terms of economic worth, the black and white male characters—Waymon, Marcus, Jay, and Hank—possess more social capital (in terms of income, residence, gender, or race) than the black females Natalie, Angela, Nina, and Leticia, who are linked by race, gender, and residential location to the African American community. However, the film narratives, through the black female protagonists, create black communities that are more agreeable to the white males Jay and Hank, who flee or avoid the white mainstream world.

Halle Berry's roles in these films indicate the latitude in black female representation in Hollywood studio productions. Black-oriented comedy–romances such as *Strictly Business* and *Boomerang* maintain the centrality of the male and his personal growth while pursuing a romance with a woman of a lower socioeconomic class. Films such as *Bulworth* and *Monster's Ball* maintain a narrative language system that presents spectacles of interracial love that are complete with atavistic images of black women in such relationships. Similar to the black males in *Strictly Business* and *Boomerang*, the white males pursue lower-class black women. An inventive woman-interested romance would establish several levels of comparative equality and not be limited to the sentimental representation of the caring and maternal lower-class female whose humanity rejuvenates the ego of a male whose social capital is not equal to or lower than the desired female. Such inventive romances will entertain and educate audiences to accept a woman who possesses more social capital than the male or, in the case of same-sex romance, acceptance of a person of color whose social capital is more than that of the white lover.

Halle Berry has become a well-respected television and movie actress who has box-office currency with black and nonblack audiences. Her career trajectory resembles that of such early black female actors as Josephine Baker, Lena Horne, Ruby Dee, Dorothy Dandridge, and Cicely Tyson, who began in black-oriented entertainment and worked their way into mainstream theater and film. Their acting talents and physical characteristics permitted them to fill supporting and leading roles in black theater and film, and then supporting roles in mainstream productions in which they were tertiary or secondary to white female leads. As long as American film studios practiced racial segregation in the writing of film scripts and the casting of screen roles, black females were limited to subservient roles that rarely permitted them sufficient frame or stage space to demonstrate their acting talents. This is also true for Halle Berry's black female contemporaries Angela Bassett, Whoopi Goldberg, Rosie Perez, Jada Pinkett Smith, Vanessa Williams, and Alfre Woodard, to mention only a few. Black actors, who receive international recognition

A very desperate black woman accepts the hospitality and love of the white man who assisted in the execution of her ex-husband: Halle Berry as Leticia and Billy Bob Thornton as Hank in Mark Forster's *Monster's Ball* (2001). (Lions Gate / The Kobal Collection / Bulliard, Jeanne Louise)

for their remarkable dramatic performances, rightly deserve the awards, regardless of the moral nature of the representative image. This is especially true for the Best Actress in a Supporting Role Oscar awardees Hattie McDaniel for *Gone with the Wind* and Whoopi Goldberg for *Ghost*, and the Best Actress Oscar awardee Halle Berry for *Monster's Ball*.

This chapter has discussed a few films that feature black women in interracial relationships with male and female nonblack lovers. Jointly, these films illustrate the open-ended forms that love takes. In considering each film's depiction of a black woman's interracial intimacy, I employ a particular type of womanist analysis that avoids a male-centric, heterosexist theoretical approach. Granted, studies of the interracial buddy films and heterosexual unions between black men and nonblack women have been helpful, but they have also created a critical vacuum because the subject was never the black female or same-sex interracial intimacy. Consequently, these studies bolster the good old boys club and deny the existence of other romantic interracial narratives.

The cinematic representation of black women has an undeniable ideological function. Filmed images form an international currency that is mutually exchanged between dominant and minority communities of film producers, studios, and filmgoers. The financial and cultural exchanges occur between developed and developing nations and leave both inevitably transformed. Films that feature black actresses in major roles function within this financial and cultural exchange medium where black womanist images bridge and traverse various national, racial, gender, and sexual borders. As discussed earlier, woman-centered films may disempower black women as *agents*.

A womanist approach to film analysis must consider the degree of agency that the black female protagonist has in work, love, and friendship. Next, the analysis should distinguish the agency of an individual black woman from the collective agency of black women as well as all women. This requires that the analysis consider how the work–love–friendship union resists, accommodates, or assimilates dominant racial, sexual, and class conventions, or how the union offers an alternative form. In responding to these questions, the analyses in this chapter show that interracial unions between black women and nonblacks sometimes maintain and other times deny the dominant atavistic images of black women and their nonblack lovers and friends. Cultural critics, film scholars, and moviegoers should realize that actors do not always find work. When actors receive roles and meet or surpass the roles' dramatic requirements, their performances deserve critical attention, rather than merely having critics note the moral or immoral nature of the character represented. Still, pressure should be directed at studios to persuade them to cast black actresses in a variety of leading and supporting roles. The next chapter considers two films by Haile Gerima, whose independent films have consistently featured black female protagonists in challenging roles that resist Hollywood binary images of black womanhood as either overweight matriarchs or brazen vixens.

NOTES

1. See Manthia Diawara, "Black Spectatorship: Problems of Identification and Resistance," *Screen* 29, no. 4 (1988): 66–81.

2. PostNegritude is an actional response to demoralizing practices that objectify individuals by limiting their identity to a singular characteristic that is naturalized as demonic, threatening, and unpatriotic.

3. Stuart Hall, "Cultural Identity and Diaspora," in *Identity: Community, Culture, Difference*, ed. Jonathan Rutherford (London: Lawrence and Wishart, 1990), 223.

4. Neal Koch, "Funny Lady, Serious Woman," *New York Times*, 24 March 2002, sec. 3, 2.

5. Koch, "Funny Lady."

6. Michel Foucault, *The Order of Things: An Archaeology of the Human Sciences* (New York: Vintage, 1973), 328.

7. See Simon Mpondo, "From Independence to Freedom: A Study of the Political Thinking of Negro-African Writers in the 1960s." Ph.D. diss., University of Washington, 1971, 1.

8. Houston A. Baker Jr., *Modernism and the Harlem Renaissance* (Chicago: University of Chicago Press, 1987), 50.

9. Frantz Fanon, *Black Skin, White Masks* (New York: Grove Weidenfeld, 1967), 188.

·6·

Black Independent Film:
Haile Gerima's *Sankofa*

$\mathcal{I}$n closing, I offer a textual analysis of two independent films by Haile Gerima and a look at the distribution strategy that Gerima used to market and exhibit *Sankofa* (Mypheduh Films, 1993) to the black American community. *Sankofa* is one example of a successfully marketed, black independent film that made a sizable profit. The receipts from the film's screenings earned Gerima sufficient money to purchase a building, which now houses a black book and video store and film-editing offices.

Sankofa's historical moment is best explained as a womanist moment in which the film attracted those black folks who are "committed to the survival and wholeness of entire people, male and female. Not a separatist, except periodically, for health."[1] The historical moment that surrounds the production, distribution, and reception of *Sankofa* is marked by the American media's interest in tragedies that produce capital. This same need kept former President Clinton in the news for all the wrong reasons. The nation's news organizations covered several violent incidents that pitted African Americans against nonblacks. Two noteworthy examples occurred in 1991. On 3 March, a group of white Los Angeles police officers—Stacey Koons, Timothy Wind, Laurence Powell, and Ted Briseno—beat African American motorist Rodney G. King while several other officers helplessly watched. In the officers' first trial, the predominantly white jury, after viewing a videotape of the beating, acquitted the officers of any unlawful use of force. Consequently, the African American and Hispanic residents in South Central Los Angeles reacted with anger and violence.

A second type of national news coverage focused on African American sports and governmental celebrities. The 11 October testimony of Anita Hill to the Senate confirmation hearings of Clarence Thomas brought black professionals and the issue of sexual harassment to the national forefront. Later during the same decade, roughly between 1994 and 1995, O. J. Simpson, a former football player who became a mediocre actor, was accused of murdering his wife, Nicole Simpson, and her male acquaintance. His spectacular L.A. freeway chase was covered by major television stations, which interrupted regular programming to follow O. J.'s escape in his white Bronco.

In all three instances, the news reports and news magazine programs focused their analysis to explain the psychology of the black individual or the black community or both. In total contrast, but perhaps just as senseless, a few blacks challenged mainstream news reports, pointing to the miscarriage of justice in the Rodney King case and the tainted evidence in the trial of O. J. Simpson as indications of a national conspiracy to emasculate or lynch black men and the African American community. When Clarence Thomas, now a U.S. Supreme Court Justice, accused the news media of giving him a "high-tech lynching," his statement validated the popular conspiracy theory that was being floated in the African American community. Clarence Thomas's Republican Party handlers wanted their man to attract the support of the black community as Rodney King had done before the American justice system. The news commentators, the conspiracy theorists, and honorable Supreme Court Justice Thomas share a similar ignorance: they never saw these as national issues—police brutality, urban riots, friendly treatment of accused murderers, and sexual harassment in U.S. government workplaces.

The L.A. uprising was an uprising of the poor who had witnessed or been a victim of police brutality. The news reporters, social commentators, and George H. W. Bush described the looters as black, which was an inaccurate description. Their hubris casts social phenomena in easily consumable, monolithic racial terms. The looters and those who tried to protect individuals from harm were multi-ethnic. They were the poor and the working poor.

A womanist postNegritude understanding of social phenomena rejects analysis that is determined by a singular or hierarchically constructed identity politics because such identity constructions maintain racial fantasies that deny the fluidity of a transracial understanding. Monolithic suffering and hierarchies of suffering obscure the reality that nonblack folk encounter police brutality, experience workplace sexual harassment, and receive less than adequate legal defense if they are poor. Additionally, it denies an opportunity for the nation to feel a common sense of shame regardless of the race, class, gender, and sexuality of the person or group. These social outrages against humanity hurt those who are against sexual harassment, police brutality, and racism; they will also return to haunt those miscreant others. Thus, in returning to the historical moment that permitted *Sankofa*'s popular reception by African Americans, the film attracted womanist folks who are "committed to the survival and wholeness of entire people, male and female. Not a separatist, except periodically, for health." These are the tenets of a womanist practice that understands that periodically one might turn inward, for psychological health. In 1993, *Sankofa* offered its viewers a moment of self-reflection and healing. The film uses a fantastic return to mother Africa to gain insight and ultimately returns its heroine to America so she can continue the good fight for all similarly oppressed communities and groups. I might even suggest that the film is very similar in intent and purpose to Michael Moore's *Fahrenheit 9/11* (Miramax, 2004) for those who opposed the reelection of George W. Bush.

The womanist wanting is not fixed to a separatist desire, but there are periodic *exceptions*, when blackness is strategically exclusive for the psychosocial health of the black community, which is in constant flux. The film offered its viewers a moment to reflect on the immediate past. It was written as a fantastic voyage to mother Africa in an effort to gain insight and, ultimately, to return to wage the good fight, which is inclusive of all similarly oppressed individuals and groups.

Haile Gerima was born in Gondar, Ethiopia, in 1946. He is the son of a writer and a teacher and the second of eight children. Although many know him as Haile, his father formally gave him the name Mypheduh, which means "sacred shield of culture" in the Ethiopian Geez language group. In 1967, he left for the United States, where he studied theater at the Goodman School of Drama in Chicago. Later, he moved to Los Angeles and enrolled in the Master of Fine Arts film production program at the University of California at Los Angeles. Presently, he is a tenured professor of film in the school of communications at Howard University in Washington, D.C., and heads Mypheduh Films, which he founded in 1982, and the Sankofa Video and Bookstore, established in 1996.

Although Gerima spent twenty-one years in Ethiopia, he identifies himself as an African filmmaker with a shared heritage with African Diaspora people. "Even if I were to return to Africa," he says, "I would always protect my direct links with black America. It has given me the courage to discover myself. . . . At first, I considered myself Ethiopian rather than connected to black America. Black America helped to humanize me."[2]

According to independent filmmaker St. Clair Bourne, Gerima's films epitomize the nonlinear black independent narrative film from the West Coast.[3] *Bush Mama* (Haile Gerima, 1976) tells the story of the awakening consciousness of Dorothy, a welfare mother whose husband is imprisoned for a crime he did not commit. Dorothy must raise her daughter in Watts, a Los Angeles inner-city neighborhood. On her return home, Dorothy discovers a white police officer attempting to rape her daughter. Like the character Sweetback, who, in Melvin Van Peebles's *Sweet Sweetback's Baadasssss Song* (Cinemation, 1971), assaults two police officers to protect Moo Moo, a young black revolutionary, Dorothy protects her next generation and kills the rapist police officer. Dorothy's violence, similar to Sweetback's, is self-protective and leads to her awakening consciousness. Although in some ways *Bush Mama* typifies the black independent family film, it is important to differentiate this film from studio-distributed black action and black family films.

First, studio-distributed black action films portray interracial violence between black and white men, while women are restricted to passive roles as sexual partners of these violent men. In contrast, Dorothy's violence protects her daughter from a sexual assault.

Second, Dorothy's violence empowers the mother–daughter relationship. This is in complete opposition to the typical Hollywood black action film, which features individualistic and masculinist-empowered heroes such as Sweetback, Shaft, and Priest, the main protagonist in *Superfly* (Warner Brothers, 1972). Unlike these black Hollywood heroes, the black independent maternal/black action hero Dorothy does not escape her socioeconomic environment through retaliatory violence or successful drug deals.

Third, unlike most studio-produced black family films, *Bush Mama* uses violence as a self-defensive action that protects and sustains the African American family. The film thereby establishes Dorothy's maternal qualities without denying the "by any means necessary" self-defensive act of violence. Her violence is restricted to one act, even though both whites and blacks constantly assault her. Here I am stressing the distinction between conventional constructions of black heroes produced for mainstream consumption and heroes such as Dorothy who are developed by independent black filmmakers. Dorothy exemplifies a black liberation hero in the way she arrives at a political consciousness that shields her daughter from further physical and sociopsychical destruction.[4]

Violent spectacles are not the central focus of *Bush Mama*, as they would have been if it were a 1975 studio-distributed black action film, or for that matter, F. Gary Gray's black female heist film *Set It Off* (New Line Cinema, 1996). Violence here merely shows that Dorothy will no longer passively endure psychological and physical abuses directed at her and her family. Dorothy becomes an agent rather than an object and a victim ripe for the pity of mainstream filmgoers who usually admit lower-class women such as Dorothy into their homes only as house cleaners and caretakers.

Though black family films, such as Daniel Petrie's *A Raisin in the Sun* (Columbia Pictures, 1961), Gordon Parks's *The Learning Tree* (Warner Brothers, 1969), Martin Ritt's *Sounder* (Twentieth Century Fox, 1972), John Berry's *Claudine* (Twentieth Century Fox, 1974), and Krishna Shah's *The River Niger* (Columbia Pictures, 1976), portray injustices, they either avoid the subject of the hero's political consciousness or limit it to static images of passivity and victimization. Black family films produced in Hollywood restrict actions to the psychological sphere. It is rare when a mainstream black-oriented film dramatizes retaliatory violence as a respectable way to resist physical threats from racist or sexist villains.

Later in this chapter, I explore how this heroic narrative form is present in Haile Gerima's *Sankofa*, which through the psychological and physical acts of Mona/Shola (played by Oyafunmike Ogunlano), develops Gerima's womanist film aesthetic of black female empowerment and can be seen as a sequel to *Bush Mama*. Mona is a twentieth-century African American fashion model, and her alter ego is Shola, who is an eighteenth-century African slave.

Many of the pre-1975 independent and black-oriented films portray heroes who nobly and selflessly endure socioeconomic hardships and sociopsychic abuses. For instance, one finds this black female type in most pre-1960 films that feature black women in major roles. Included in this group are such actresses and films as Abbey Lincoln in Michael Roemer's *Nothing But a Man* (Cinema V, 1964), Cicely Tyson in Leo Penn's *A Man Called Adam* (Embassy Pictures, 1966), and Tyson in later roles in *Sounder* (1972) and *Claudine* (1974).

In contrast, Gerima's *Bush Mama* suggests a black hero who proudly endures dehumanizing situations but should not be idolized. As its screenwriter and director, Gerima resists conventional closure that would reunite Dorothy's family or would permit her to escape her socioeconomic conditions. Through his film, Gerima expresses the view that permanent changes in the social system will not result from a fictional narrative. True, Dorothy retaliates against black-on-black crime, insensitive welfare workers, and police brutality. But Gerima insists that her struggle be against institutions, such as the welfare office and the police force, rather than representatives acting in their name. The independent film praxis of Gerima's generation of black filmmakers requires a resolute struggle against the classical Hollywood narrative form and its bourgeois ideological content.

Consequently, *Bush Mama*'s nonlinear narrative style, apparent in the use of collage and abrupt editing, evokes a self-reflexive form that disrupts the spectator's pleasurable identification with story and protagonist, thereby refusing the relationship that the film spectator has with classical Hollywood narratives. Charles Burnett, Larry Clark, and Alile Sharon Larkin use this technique for similar political purposes. Avant-garde and experimental camera techniques deter the recurrent critical and spectator relationships that classical narratives usually enjoy.[5]

It is advantageous for a filmmaker to attract large audiences by manipulating various styles—classical, avant-garde, and experimental—to produce an interesting cinematic form while still articulating politically sensitive but appropriate issues and themes. Like most audiences, regardless of their ethnicity, the largest black audiences grew up consuming dominant narrative forms and stereotypes of themselves and others. Later, I will discuss the manner in which Gerima's *Sankofa* displays a syncretic film style that engages elements of the classical, avant-garde, and experimental styles.[6]

In 1973, Gerima began the production of *Bush Mama*, and by 1976 he had received the finished print. Since the demise of the West Coast–based Lincoln Motion Picture Company, *Bush Mama* became one of the first West Coast features, if not the first feature, that was produced, directed, edited, and personally distributed by a university-trained black independent filmmaker. *Bush Mama*, Charles Burnett's *Killer of Sheep* (1977), Larry Clark's *Passing Through* (1977), and Julie Dash's *Illusions* (1983) typify the new black independent features made on the West Coast in the late 1970s and early 1980s. During the early 1990s, Burnett,

Dash, Gerima, and a 1980s generation of university-trained black film-makers such as John Singleton used different modes of production and distribution to produce a distinctly blues-inflected African American cinema. Many of their films exhibit a slow pacing owing to the use of long-duration shots and minimal editing. I am thinking in particular of Burnett's *To Sleep with Anger* (Columbia Pictures, 1990), Dash's *Daughters of the Dust* (Kino, 1991), Singleton's *Boyz N the Hood* (Columbia Pictures, 1991), and Gerima's *Sankofa* (1993).

Sweet Sweetback's Baadasssss Song (Cinemation, 1971) established a new heroic paradigm for the black cinematic hero as sexual, individualistic, and violent. However, Sweetback's violent actions haphazardly connect him to a young black radical. His individualism links him to the black community, while his sexual activity is a tool used to escape life-threatening encounters. *Sweetback* and other similarly produced and distributed black independent films provide instances when a sociocultural moment permits the necessary free zone for certain independent film-makers to successfully produce and distribute their films. Van Peebles's

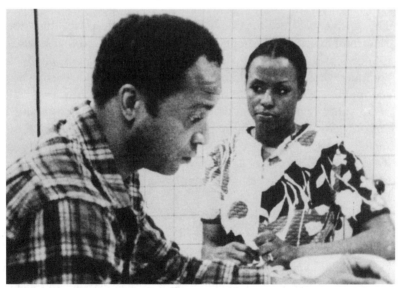

The distraught looks of a hardworking black couple living in the Watts neighborhood of Los Angeles are quite telling; this family endures stoically: Henry Gayle Sanders as Stan and Kaycee Moore as his wife in Charles Burnett's *Killer of Sheep* (1977), which was selected for the National Film Registry in 1990. (The Kobal Collection)

film attracted a large black following whose more radical members had opposing attitudes toward the film and its hero.[7] In the 1990s, Julie Dash's *Daughters* and Haile Gerima's *Sankofa* garnered similar marketing successes and popularity with black audiences. Unlike *Sweetback*, the two films are black female centered. *Daughters* enjoyed a degree of success in its marketing and reception similar to the other two films.

In 1993, Gerima produced and directed a notable contribution to black film history. Using the marketing and distribution strategies of the earliest black independents, Gerima successfully marketed and distributed *Sankofa*. The film grossed more than two and a half million dollars.[8] Gerima's marketing success with *Sankofa* showed once more that a truly independently produced and distributed black film could be successfully marketed to large audiences, if the story addressed the sociocultural and psychological needs of its people. Dialogic zones of free exchange exist and are in constant flux and can enable formerly silenced discourses.

ONE MUST RETURN TO THE PAST IN ORDER TO MOVE FORWARD

The word *sankofa* derives from an Akan West African word meaning "one must return to the past in order to move forward"; the sankofa bird is known as the "bird of passage." In this film, Sankofa is the divine drummer whose rhythmic drumbeats and voice-over guide the narrative and the protagonist. In Akan religious lore, Sankofa is also viewed as a divine entity. In the film *Sankofa*, the "return to the past in order to move forward" has the main protagonist, Mona, a twentieth-century African American fashion model, become Shola, an eighteenth-century African slave. Mona, as Shola, endures the Middle Passage and returns with an enlightened black consciousness, similar to what happens to the hero Dorothy in *Bush Mama*.

The film opens with drumbeats over images of African art objects and the credit sequence. A medium close-up of a wooden sankofa bird appears as the drumming continues and a Sankofa-like voice-over monologue begins: "Spirits of the dead rise up, lingering spirits of the dead rise up . . . and possess your vessel. Those Africans shackled in leg irons and enslaved, step out of the acres of cane fields and cotton fields and tell your story. Those lynched in the magnolias, swinging on the limbs of weeping willows, rotting food for the vultures, step down and claim your story. Those tied, bound, and whipped from Brazil to Mississippi. Those in Jamaica, in the fields of Cuba, in the swamps of Florida, the rice fields of Carolina, you waiting Africans step out and tell your story." Crosscutting between the cane fields and Sankofa (Kofi Ghanaba), the divine drummer visually enhances the monologue and cinematically introduces Gerima's compelling story about the African holocaust. The repeating image of a buzzard and Sankofa's rhythmic drumming connect to a series of visually stunning medium close-ups of the white-powdered drummer who implores us with "Africa, listen."

The next shot presents a contemporary African coastal area with busy anglers. The shot that follows contrasts with the preceding naturalistic images of the African coast. It shows Mona, a scantily clad black female, posing in a swimsuit as a white male photographer goads her to pose in a more erotic manner. A tall, slender, middle-aged African man holding a wooden sankofa staff looks angrily at them and frightens Mona. This man is the human equivalent of Sankofa, as is the African drummer whose drumbeats and chants introduce the film. The next scenes establish Mona's centrality to the African holocaust narrative by showing her branded and chained in the Cape Coast Castle dungeon. She cries to her captors, "Wait a minute! You're making a mistake. Don't you recognize me? I'm Mona. I'm an American!" This fact is lost on her captors, who confine her with the other slaves. The historical time has shifted and the slavers hold Mona captive in the dungeon of the castle. She must now honor the drummer Sankofa's earlier admonishment "Africa, listen." The film thus begins its story of Mona's African American double, Shola, a house servant who was born on the Lafayette sugarcane plantation. Shola's master constantly rapes her, and when she looks to the Catholic priest, Father Raphael (Reginald Carter), for spiritual help, he tells her to seek refuge in prayer. Her lover Shango (Mutabaruka; Shango is the name of a Santeria god), an Afro-Caribbean field slave, entreats her to reject Christianity and accept African spirituality. Shango argues that the white man's religion does not offer an escape from rapes and physical enslavement. After Shola accepts African spirituality, Shango offers her a carved wooden sankofa bird that his father had given him. This weds the two, Shango and Shola, and leads to Shola's physical return to Africa and Mona's spiritual return to her African roots. In a voice-over narrative accompanied by a chanting chorus and crane shots moving over cane fields and a large body of water, Shola describes her spiritual passage from slavery to freedom.

"Guns, Horses, Head Slaves, I can still hear it all now. I heard the guns go off again. The dogs, I heard them as they scrunched one of us. I heard his voice. Keep runnin' sister. Suddenly I heard another one go down. They were right on our heels. I knew I was next. One cried out to me to go on as the dogs feasted on him. Keep runnin' sister. Then I had this feelin', this light feelin'. And there wasn't no more pains in my feet. This big buzzard was flyin' next to me and he spread his wings and scooped me up and up. Just like what Shango said. The buzzard brought me."

Mona as Shola must witness the humiliation and physical abuse that most, if not all, African slave women experienced in the New World. The final sequence presents Mona in African garb. She walks out of the dungeon and joins the black people who sit observing the performance of the white-powdered Sankofa drummer chanting the "Spirits of the Dead" monologue that introduced the film.

SANKOFA: PRODUCTION, DISTRIBUTION, AND EXHIBITION

Initially, American film distributors and theaters refused to market Gerima's *Sankofa*. As Oscar Micheaux had done more than seventy years before him, Gerima carried his film throughout the United States and offered screenings accompanied by lectures. He screened *Sankofa* in churches, community spaces, and rented theaters. He traveled to thirty-five cities and received a healthy box office for his efforts. "Churches and schools came in busloads to see *Sankofa*," Gerima reports. He understood this attraction for his film as reflecting a desire for films that are rarely available to the black community:

> Most black movies make black people look very bizarre, hope-lessly bizarre; this is unacceptable. Commercial filmmakers some-times leave the community unfulfilled and demoralized, asking itself: "Is this all that blacks are capable of?" Church people com-plain that the romanticism and glamour associated with violence in mainstream black films trickle back into the community. While Hollywood continues to select and produce films that reflect its own view of what the black community is, this contradiction will continue.[9]

Gerima faced local and international rebuffs when seeking financing and distribution for *Sankofa*. Gerima called these instances censorship at the pre- and postproduction phase:

> In America, slavery is a very sensitive topic. The moment I wanted to make *Sankofa* (1993), my credentials in the USA vanished because I was venturing into forbidden territory. The resource centers were closed to me. I couldn't get funding. Censorship became a reality; the funding agencies for cultural development shut their doors. They'd talk about timing: "this year's budget is nearly spent. You're too late or too early." Nobody comes out with it straight and says that the subject matter is wrong. The press is much the same; they wouldn't touch *Sankofa* at Berlin, though it was in competition with big budget movies. They censor you by making you non-existent. We went to Montreal and Toronto [in September 1993]: they skipped us, didn't even talk to us. They thought we were finished.[10]

According to Gerima, the international press that covered film festivals in Berlin, Montreal, and Toronto in 1993 avoided discussing his film. He took their rebuff as a form of censorship that made his film nonexistent to distributors and potential audiences. He readily acknowledges that the subject matter of slavery is a topic that is rarely welcomed, and even less so when he films it in a particularly nonclassical style. Although Steven Spielberg's *Amistad* treated a similar history and had lackluster box-office receipts, it did have the benefit of a linear narrative that appealed to audiences versed in classical narrative film style. Because of Spielberg's power within the film industry, his film also enjoyed wide domestic and international distribution and press coverage. This was certainly not the case with Gerima's *Sankofa* or any other of his eight feature films. Thus, for some, *Sankofa*'s remarkable box-office success might be cause for optimism about the future of black independent filmmaking, but it is an optimism that I do not share. One reason is that multinational companies that have little interest in the visual arts control film production, distribution, and exhibition. Their control of the market leaves little room for independent filmmakers such as Gerima. Another is that several critically successful black independent filmmakers, such as Julie Dash, Cheryl Dunye, and Charles Burnett, to mention just a few, have one independently produced and widely distributed film that has become a singular success story that is not repeated. For the most part, black independent filmmakers are relegated to film festivals and college campuses. Thus, the public has no knowledge of this black film culture, its alternative narrative styles, and the sociopolitical world that many of its films explore.

Although some critics might find that *Sankofa*'s sentimentality closely resembles contemporary classical Hollywood melodramas, black communities celebrated the film as a genuine articulation of the African Diaspora holocaust. Black audiences packed its various premieres. Still, no U.S. distributors were interested. Undaunted by the cold reception his film received from the press and distributors, Gerima invited twenty Washington, D.C., activists to open a local theater for regular screenings of the film. After *Sankofa*'s box-office receipts established it as a popular film with the local black community, the New York Cineplex Theatre signed a rental agreement.

In 1995, United Artist Theatres distributed and screened *Sankofa* on the West Coast. For some unexplained reason, the UA Theatres scheduled for Sankofa deteriorated into irregular screenings in smaller rooms. Consequently, much of the film's potential audience was discouraged by the irregularities and limited available seating, and only the most courageous and flexible filmgoer got to see the film during its three-week engagement. After the UA debacle, the Magic Johnson Theatres booked *Sankofa* for the rest of that summer, with regular screenings in spacious rooms. Magic Johnson Theatres is a Los Angeles, black-owned, and black-operated theater chain that exhibits black-oriented films as well as Hollywood mainstream fare. According to Eric Martin, the manager at Magic Johnson Theatres, the daily grosses outperformed Danny Cannon's *Judge Dredd* (Buena Vista Pictures, 1995) and Ron Howard's *Apollo 13* (Universal Pictures, 1995), which were also being shown at the theater.

Nevertheless, the Blockbuster video chain, one of the largest and certainly the most important video distribution chain in the United States, would not stock *Sankofa*. Again, Gerima was undaunted. He took the profits he had made from the theatrical distribution of *Sankofa* and made a down payment on a building in which he opened Sankofa Video and Bookstore. The building also has conference rooms and postproduction facilities. It was here that Shirikiana Aina, Gerima's wife and the vice president of Mypheduh Films, edited her first feature-length film, *Through the Door of No Return* (Mypheduh Films, 1997). In 1999, Gerima used the editing facilities for his next feature film, *Adwa*.¹¹ Gerima observes:

> Many African-Americans and Chicanos can't make the movies they want to make, because they don't live up to the expectations of white producers. That's why you see so many black independent film-makers playing [*sic*] in with Hollywood and making bizarre "shoot 'em up and kill" movies. Black people respect Spike Lee, especially for his shrewd ability to function in that mega world; he brings many black talents into his productions. Our people see Spike walking the commercial tightrope to make something serious, and more dignified. He's at a critical stage now, and we are waiting to see what happens next. . . . *Sankofa* may well be a milestone linking African cinema to African-American cinema. It is the first time two [West] African countries, Ghana and Burkina Faso, have collaborated on a film about slavery. But to talk of African cinema is sometimes very hard: even Ousmane Sembene, the father of African social cinema, has to wait 10 to 15 years between films, and I know 20 film-makers in Ethiopia who have not made a film in five years.¹²

Haile Gerima's twenty-five-plus-year career as an independent filmmaker, producer, and distributor-owner of Mypheduh Films provides American film history and world cinema with a fertile example of the limits of multinational capitalism and mainstream tastes. Although the earlier film and distribution career of William Greaves might seem as important, if not more important, to any discussion of black independent cinema, Gerima's case offers other important details.¹³ Through his Mypheduh Films, Gerima controls the production and distribution of his films and works by other African and African Diaspora artists, and as a tenured professor of film, he has been the mentor of future filmmakers and film scholars who attend Howard University. His international reputation as an independent filmmaker, producer, and writer makes him a formidable example of what consistency and purpose can accomplish. His work consistently expresses a distinct type of womanist ethics and is a worthy subject of any discussion of independent American cinema. In studying Gerima's experiences in marketing his films in the United States, one sees the layers of institutional racism and other problems that American-based independent filmmakers face. Gerima's case is of singular importance in that, for almost three decades, he has steadily worked in the independent film arena and steadfastly made films that express a womanist ethics of black female empowerment. In making *Bush Mama*, he became the first member of the Los Angeles-based, university-trained group to produce an independent feature film that helped to establish a womanist, independent film practice. Almost twenty years later, his fifth feature, *Sankofa*, took *Bush Mama*'s womanist hero to her Afrocentric roots and returned her with an enriched and empowered African American consciousness. Malcolm Little's travels as Malcolm X to African nations and his pilgrimage to Mecca equal the imaginative and spiritual travels of Mona as the enslaved, then liberated, Shola.

NOTES

1. Alice Walker, *In Search of Our Mothers' Gardens: Womanist Prose by Alice Walker* (New York: Harcourt Brace Jovanovich, 1983), xi. Also see Sherley Anne Williams, "Some Implications of Womanist Theory," in *Reading Black, Reading Feminist*, ed. Henry Louis Gates Jr., 68–75 (New York: Meridian, 1990).

2. Louis Marcorelles, "Haile Gerima: 'J'appartiens à la fois à l'Éthiopie et à l'Amérique noire,'" *Le Monde*, 7 July 1984, 11(N).

3. St. Clair Bourne, "Black Film Movement," in *Black Cinema Aesthetics: Issues in Independent Black Filmmaking*, ed. Gladstone L. Yearwood (Athens: Ohio University Center for Afro-American Studies, 1982), 104–105.

4. Gerima says: "If I was interested in her violent act, the next logical scene would be prison. . . . However, the stages of her assertion were more entertaining. In the first stage of her consciousness, a young person snatches her purse. She is incapable of even defending her purse from a little kid. The second stage is the oppressive woman who represents the state [a clerk at the welfare agency] and commits silent violence against her; Dorothy retaliates in fantasy by breaking a bottle over the woman's head. The third level was when it affected her daughter. My obsessive theme deals with consciousness. . . . When do you begin to become aware of the fact that the world has to be changed, and what are the processes that lead towards that awareness? For Dorothy, [it was] when the oppressive tool came down on her daughter. . . . She stood her ground and asserted herself in very physical terms. . . . [I]t is with her consciousness that I ended the film and not at the logical conclusion of a conventional drama that would show that she went to jail." Steve Howard, "A Cinema of Transformation: The Films of Haile Gerima," *Cineaste* 14 (May 1985): 29.

5. Gerima says (my translation): "Conventional film narrative techniques say that we cannot express ourselves cinematically as we would normally do. The cinematographic rules and aesthetic principals of the classical film narrative determine what

films are well crafted. Independent filmmakers should resist conforming to the dictates of the dominant film form and aesthetic values of Hollywood. Black cinema should be judged by blacks' particular sociocultural experience. The struggle should not be limited to aesthetical questions but must include the business of film distribution and exhibition." ("Le cinéma conventionnel dit qu'on ne peut pas s'exprimer tel que nous avons l'habitude de le faire. Cette dictature implique qu'il y a seulement un langage cinématographique et un tempérament cinématographique. Nous avons donc une responsabilité linguistique. Si on perpétue cet Hollywood monolithique, cette règle d'un langage pour tout le monde, le cinéma ne représente aucun intérêt pour moi. Le cinéma Noir sera jugé et évalué selon le baromètre des Anglo-Saxons. Il ne s'agit pas seulement de ne pas accepter les conventions: la lutte doit porter sur le médium lui-même.") Yann Lardeau, "Haile Gerima: Pour un mouvement de libération culturelle," *Le Monde Diplomatique* 364 (July 1984), 5(N).

6. "The issue is not the expression of some lost origin or some uncontaminated essence in black film language, but the adoption of a critical 'voice' that promotes consciousness of the collision of cultures and histories that constitutes our very conditions of existence." Kobena Mercer, "Diaspora Culture and the Dialogic Imagination: The Aesthetics of Black Independent Film in Britain," in *The Media Reader*, ed. Manuel Alvarado and John O. Thompson (London: British Film Institute, 1990), 24–25.

7. See Mark A. Reid, *Redefining Black Film* (Berkeley: University of California Press, 1993), 77–83.

8. Jesse Algeron Rhines, *Black Film/White Money* (New Brunswick, NJ: Rutgers University Press, 1996), 171.

9. "Haile Gerima Images of Africa," *Index on Censorship* 6 (1995), at www .oneworld.org/index_oc/issue695/hailegerima.html (accessed 11 August 2001).

10. "Haile Gerima Images of Africa."

11. Esther Iverem, "Blackbuster: Haile Gerima's D.C. Store Rents a Different Kind of Black Film," *Seeing Black* (2001), at www.seeingblack.com/x040901/sanko fa.shtml (accessed 6 September 2001).

12. "Haile Gerima Images of Africa."

13. On Greaves, see Reid, *Redefining Black Film*, 126–27.

Bibliography

Ames, Christopher. "Restoring the Black Man's Lethal Weapon: Race and Sexuality in Contemporary Cop Films." *Journal of Popular Film and Television* 20, no. 3 (1992): 60–62.

Baker, Houston A., Jr. *Modernism and the Harlem Renaissance.* Chicago: University of Chicago Press, 1987.

Blumenfeld, Samuel. "J'étais fier de posséder une culture noire." Interview with Quentin Tarantino. *Le Monde*, 4 February 1998, 31.

———. "Blaxploitation, le cinéma du ghetto." *Le Monde*, 31 March 1998, 28.

Bobo, Jacqueline. *Black Women as Cultural Readers.* New York: Columbia University Press, 1995.

Bourne, St. Clair. "Black Film Movement." In *Black Cinema Aesthetics: Issues in Independent Black Filmmaking*, edited by Gladstone L. Yearwood, 93–105. Athens: Ohio University Center for Afro-American Studies, 1982.

Boyd, Todd. *Am I Black Enough for You?: Popular Culture from the Hood and Beyond.* Bloomington: Indiana University Press, 1997.

Burnett, Charles. "Inner City Blues." In *Questions of Third Cinema*, edited by Jim Pines and Paul Willemen, 223–26. London: British Film Institute, 1989.

Butters, Gerald R., Jr. *Black Manhood on the Silent Screen.* Lawrence: University Press of Kansas, 2002.

Carson, Diane, Linda Dittmar, and Janice Welsch, eds. *Multiple Voices in Feminist Film Criticism.* Minneapolis: University of Minnesota Press, 1994.

Cham, Mbye, and Claire Andrade-Watkins, eds. *Blackframes: Critical Perspectives on Black Independent Cinema.* Cambridge: MIT Press, 1988.

Creed, Barbara. "Kristeva, Femininity, Abjection." In *The Horror Reader*, edited by E. Ken Gelder, 64–70. New York: Routledge, 2000.

Cripps, Thomas. *Slow Fade to Black: The Negro in American Film, 1900–1942.* New York: Oxford University Press, 1977.

———. *Making Movies Black: The Hollywood Message Movie from World War II to the Civil Rights Era.* New York: Oxford University Press, 1993.

Depestre, René. *Bonjour et adieu à la négritude, suivi de Travaux D'identité.* Paris: Seghers, 1980.

Diawara, Manthia. "Black Spectatorship: Problems of Identification and Resistance." *Screen* 29, no. 4 (1988): 66–81.

———. "Noir by Noirs: Toward a New Realism in Black Cinema." *African American Review* 27, no. 4 (1993): 525–38.

———, ed. *Black American Cinema.* New York: Routledge, 1993.

Dickerson, Ernest. Interview in "Diggin' Up *Bones*" (2002) and "Urban Gothic" (2002) on *Bones,* DVD, 2002.

Dickson, Lynda Fae. "The Early Club Movement among Black Women in Denver, 1890–1925." Ph.D. diss., University of Colorado, 1982.

Durham, Philip, and Everett L. Jones. *The Negro Cowboys.* New York: Dodd, Mead, 1965.

Fanon, Frantz. *Black Skin, White Masks.* New York: Grove Weidenfeld, 1967.

Foucault, Michel. *The History of Sexuality.* Vol. 1: An Introduction. Trans. Robert Hurley. New York: Vintage, 1980.

Friedman, Lester D. "*Canyons of Nightmare*: The Jewish Horror Film." In *Planks of Reason: Essays on the Horror Film,* edited by Barry Keith Grant, 126–52. Metuchen, NJ: Scarecrow, 1984.

Friedman, Milton. "There's No Justice in the War on Drugs." *New York Times,* 1 November 1998, Op-Ed, 19.

Gates, Henry Louis, Jr., ed. *Reading Black, Reading Feminist.* New York: Meridian, 1990.

George, Nelson. *Blackface: Reflections on African-Americans and the Movies.* New York: HarperCollins, 1994.

Gerima, Haile. "Haile Gerima Images of Africa." *Index on Censorship 6.* 1995. At www.oneworld.org/index_oc/issue695/hailegerima.html (accessed 11 August 2001).

Gonzalez, Ed. "Bones." *Slant Magazine,* 2001. At www.slantmagazine.com/film/film_review.asp?ID = 58 (accessed 31 March 2003).

Gooding-Williams, Robert, ed. *Reading Rodney King, Reading Urban Uprising.* New York: Routledge, 1993.

Gray, Herman. "Black Masculinity and Visual Culture." In *Black Male: Representations of Masculinity in Contemporary American Art,* edited by Thelma Golden, 175–80. New York: Whitney Museum of American Art, 1994.

Grinde, Donald A., Jr., and Quintard Taylor. "Red v. Black: Conflict and Accommodation in the Post Civil War Indian Territory, 1865–1907." *American Indian Quarterly* 8 (1984): 211–25.

Guerrero, Ed. *Framing Blackness: The African American Image in Film.* Philadelphia: Temple University Press, 1993.

Hall, Stuart. "Cultural Identity and Cinematic Representation." *Framework* 6 (1989): 68–81.

Hardy, Ernest. "I, Too, Sing Hollywood: Four Women on Race, Art and Making Movies." *L.A. Weekly*, 20–26, October 2000. At www.laweekly.com/ink/00/48/cover-hardy1.shtml (accessed 23 October 2000).

Harper, Philip Brian. "Walk-on Parts and Speaking Subjects: Screen Representations of Black Gay Men." In *Black Male: Representations of Masculinity in Contemporary American Art*, edited by Thelma Golden, 141–48. New York: Whitney Museum of American Art, 1994.

Harrington, Richard. "Def by Temptation." *Washington Post*, 5 June 1990. At www.washingtonpost.com/wp-srv/style/longterm/movies/videos/defbytemptationrharrington_a0aae9.htm (accessed 31 March 2003).

Harris, Trudier. "On *The Color Purple*, Stereotypes, and Silence." *Black American Literature Forum* 18 (1984): 155–61.

hooks, bell. *Black Looks: Race and Representation*. Boston: South End, 1992.

Howard, Steve. "A Cinema of Transformation: The Films of Haile Gerima." Interview with Haile Gerima. *Cineaste* 14 (May 1985): 28, 29, 39.

Hunt, Leon. "A Sadistic Night at the Opera." In *The Horror Reader*, edited by E. Ken Gelder, 324–35. New York: Routledge, 2000.

Iverem, Esther. "Blackbuster: Haile Gerima's D.C. Store Rents a Different Kind of Black Film." *Seeing Black*. 2001. At www.seeingblack.com/x040901/sankofa.shtml (accessed 6 September 2001).

Johnson, Albert. "Beige, Brown or Black." *Film Quarterly* 13 (Fall 1959).

Journal of Communication Inquiry 10 (Summer 1986).

Kellner, Douglas. *Media Culture: Cultural Studies, Identity and Politics between the Modern and Postmodern*. London: Routledge, 1995.

Klotman, Phyllis R. *Screenplays of the African American Experience*. Bloomington: Indiana University Press, 1991.

———, ed. *African Americans in Cinema: The First Half-Century*. CD-ROM. Champaign: University of Illinois Press, 2003.

Klotman, Phyllis R., and Janet K. Cutler, eds. *Struggles for Representation: African American Documentary Film and Video*. Bloomington: Indiana University Press, 1999.

Kristeva, Julia. *Powers of Horror: An Essay on Abjection*. Trans. Leon S. Roudiez. New York: Columbia University Press, 1982.

Lapp, Rudolph. *Blacks in the Gold Rush*. New Haven: Yale University Press, 1977.

Lardeau, Yann. "Haile Gerima: Pour un mouvement de libération culturelle." Interview with Haile Gerima. *Le Monde Diplomatique* 364 (July 1984), 5(N).

Lott, Tommy L. "A No-Theory Theory of Contemporary Black Cinema." *Black American Literature Forum* 25, no. 2 (1991): 221–36.

Lowry, Ed, and Richard deCordova. "Enunciation and the Production of Horror in *White Zombie*." In *Planks of Reason: Essays on the Horror Film*, edited by Barry Keith Grant, 346–89. Metuchen, NJ: Scarecrow, 1984.

Marcorelles, Louis. "Haile Gerima: 'J'appartiens à la fois à l'Éthiopie et à l'Amérique noire.'" Interview with Haile Gerima. *Le Monde*, 7 July 1984, 11(N).

Mayne, Judith. *Cinema and Spectatorship.* New York: Routledge, 1993.

Mercer, Kobena. "Diaspora Culture and the Dialogic Imagination: The Aesthetics of Black Independent Film in Britain." In *The Media Reader*, edited by Manuel Alvarado and John O. Thompson, 24–35. London: British Film Institute, 1990.

Needham, Gary. "Playing with Genre: An Introduction to the Italian *Giallo.*" In *Fear without Frontiers: Horror Cinema across the Globe*, ed. Steven Jay Schneider, 135–44. Godalming, England: FAB, 2003.

Nichols, Peter M. "Climbing toward the Domain of the Independent Movie Elite." *New York Times*, 1 April 1998, sec. 2, 26.

Nowell-Smith, Geoffrey. "The Beautiful and the Bad: Notes on Some Actorial Stereotypes." In *Hollywood and Europe: Economics, Culture, National Identity, 1945–1995*, edited by Geoffrey Nowell-Smith and Steven Ricci, 135–41. London: British Film Institute, 1998.

Porter, Kenneth W. "Negro Labor in the Western Cattle Industry, 1866–1900." *Labor History* 10 (1969): 346–64, 366–68, 370–74.

Ray, Robert B. *A Certain Tendency of the Hollywood Cinema, 1930–1980.* Princeton, NJ: Princeton University Press, 1985.

Reid, Mark, Janine Euvrard, Francis Bordat, and Raphaël Bassan, eds. *Le cinéma noir américain.* Paris: CinémAction/Cerf, 1988.

Reid, Mark A. "The Achievement of Oscar Micheaux." *Black Film Review* 4, no. 2 (Spring 1988): 7.

———. *Redefining Black Film.* Berkeley: University of California Press, 1993.

———. "The Black Gangster Film." In *Film Genre Reader II*, edited by Barry Keith Grant, 456–73. Austin: University of Texas Press, 1995.

———. *PostNegritude Visual and Literary Culture.* Albany: State University of New York Press, 1997.

———, ed. *Spike Lee's "Do the Right Thing."* New York: Cambridge University Press, 1997.

Rhines, Jesse Algeron. *Black Film/White Money.* New Brunswick, NJ: Rutgers University Press, 1996.

Sampson, Henry T. *Blacks in Black and White: A Source Book on Black Films.* Metuchen, NJ: Scarecrow, 1977.

Sanjek, David. "Fan's Notes: The Horror Film Fanzine." In *The Horror Reader*, edited by E. Ken Gelder, 314–23. New York: Routledge, 2000.

Scheib, Richard. "Bones." *Rotten Tomatoes* (2001). At www.rottentomatoes.com (accessed 31 March 2003).

Smith, Barbara. "Towards a Black Feminist Criticism." In *The New Feminist Criticism*, edited by Elaine Showalter, 4–18. New York: Pantheon, 1985.

Staiger, Janet. *Interpreting Films: Studies in the Historical Reception of American Cinema.* Princeton, NJ: Princeton University Press, 1992.

Taylor, Clyde R. "Decolonizing the Image: New U.S. Black Cinema." *Jump Cut* (1985): 166–78.

————. "The LA Rebellion: New Spirit in American Film." *Black Film Review* 2 (1986): 2.

————. *The Mask of Art: Breaking the Aesthetic Contract: Film and Literature.* Bloomington: Indiana University Press, 1998.

Tolson, Arthur L. *The Black Oklahomans: A History, 1541–1972.* New Orleans: Edwards Print Co., 1972.

Walker, Alice. *In Search of Our Mothers' Gardens: Womanist Prose by Alice Walker.* New York: Harcourt Brace Jovanovich, 1983.

Waller, Gregory A. "Introduction to American Horrors." In *The Horror Reader,* edited by Ken Gelder, 256–64. New York: Routledge, 2000.

Watkins, Mel. "Sexism, Racism and Black Women Writers." *New York Times Book Review,* 6 December 1986, 1, 35–37.

Watkins, S. Craig. *Representing: Hip Hop Culture and the Production of Black Cinema.* Chicago: University of Chicago Press, 1998.

Wilson, William Julius. *The Truly Disadvantaged: The Inner City, the Underclass, and Public Policy.* Chicago: University of Chicago Press, 1987.

Wood, Robin. "Introduction to the American Horror Film." In *Planks of Reason: Essays on the Horror Film,* edited by Barry Keith Grant, 164–200. Metuchen, NJ: Scarecrow, 1984.

Yearwood, Gladstone, ed. *Black Cinema Aesthetics: Issues in Independent Black Filmmaking.* Athens: Ohio University Center for Afro-American Studies, 1982.

————. *Black Film as a Signifying Practice: Cinema, Narration and the African-American Aesthetic Tradition.* Trenton, NJ: Africa World, 2000.

Young, Elizabeth. "Here Comes the Bride: Wedding, Gender and Race in *Bride of Frankenstein.*" In *The Horror Reader,* edited by Ken Gelder, 128–42. New York: Routledge, 2000.

Zavarzadeh, Mas'ud. *Seeing Films Politically.* Albany: State University of New York Press, 1991.

Zimmerman, Bonnie. "Daughters of Darkness: The Lesbian Vampire on Film." In *Planks of Reason: Essays on the Horror Film,* edited by Barry Keith Grant, 153–63. Metuchen, NJ: Scarecrow, 1984.

Selected Filmography

MAJOR AND MINI STUDIO–DISTRIBUTED
AFRICAN AMERICAN FILMS, 1990 TO 2001

1990

Def by Temptation (Troma Films, 1990, James Bond III)
House Party (Columbia Pictures, 1990, Reginald Hudlin)
Mo' Better Blues (Universal Pictures, 1990, Spike Lee)
To Sleep with Anger (Columbia Pictures, 1990, Charles Burnett)

1991

Boyz N the Hood (Columbia Pictures, 1991, John Singleton)
Daughters of the Dust (Kino, 1991, Julie Dash)
The Five Heartbeats (Twentieth Century Fox, 1991, Robert Townsend)
House Party II (Avco-Embassy, 1991, George Jackson and Doug McHenry)
Jungle Fever (Universal Pictures, 1991, Spike Lee)
New Jack City (Warner Brothers, 1991, Mario Van Peebles)
One False Move (I.R.S. Media International, 1991, Carl Franklin)
Straight Out of Brooklyn (Samuel Goldwyn, 1991, Matty Rich)
Strictly Business (Warner Brothers, 1991, Kevin Hooks)

1992

Boomerang (Paramount, 1992, Reginald Hudlin)
Deep Cover (New Line Cinema, 1992, Bill Duke)
Juice (Paramount, 1992, Ernest Dickerson)
Malcolm X (Warner Brothers, 1992, Spike Lee)

1993

CB4 (Universal Pictures, 1993, Tamra Davis)
Just Another Girl on the I.R.T. (Miramax, 1993, Leslie Harris)
Menace II Society (New Line Cinema, 1993, Allen and Albert Hughes)
Poetic Justice (Columbia Pictures, 1993, John Singleton)
Posse (Polygram, 1993, Mario Van Peebles)
Sankofa (Mypheduh Films, 1993, Haile Gerima)

1994

Crooklyn (Universal Pictures, 1994, Spike Lee)
House Party III (New Line Cinema, 1994, Eric Meza)
I Like It Like That (Columbia Pictures, 1994, Darnell Martin)
The Inkwell (Buena Vista Pictures, 1994, Matty Rich)
Jason's Lyric (Polygram, 1994, Doug McHenry)
Sugar Hill a.k.a. *Harlem* (Twentieth Century Fox, 1994, Leon Ichaso)

1995

Clockers (Universal Pictures, 1995, Spike Lee)
Dead Presidents (Buena Vista Pictures, 1995, Allen and Albert Hughes)
Devil in a Blue Dress (TriStar Pictures, 1995, Carl Franklin)
Fear of a Black Hat (Savoy Pictures, 1995, Rusty Cundieff)
Friday (New Line Cinema, 1995, F. Gary Gray)
The Glass Shield (Miramax, 1995, Charles Burnett)
Higher Learning (Columbia Pictures, 1995, John Singleton)
Love Jones (New Line Cinema, 1995, Theodore Witcher)
Once Upon a Time When We Were Colored (BET Pictures, 1995, Tim Reid)
Panther (Polygram, 1995, Mario Van Peebles)
Tales from the Hood (Savoy Pictures, 1995, Rusty Cundieff)
Waiting to Exhale (Twentieth Century Fox, 1995, Forest Whitaker)
The Walking Dead (Savoy Pictures, 1995, Preston A. Whitmore II)

1996

The Associate (Buena Vista Pictures, 1996, Donald Petrie)
Don't Be a Menace to South Central While Drinking Your Juice in the Hood (Miramax, 1996, Paris Barclay)
Girl 6 (Twentieth Century Fox, 1996, Spike Lee)
Original Gangstas (Orion Pictures, 1996, Larry Cohen; Fred Williamson, producer)

Set It Off (New Line Cinema, 1996, F. Gary Gray)
The Watermelon Woman (First Run Features, 1996, Cheryl Dunye)

1997

Eve's Bayou (Trimark, 1997, Kasi Lemmons)
Get On the Bus (Columbia Pictures, 1997, Spike Lee)
Gridlock'd (Polygram, 1997, Vondie Curtis-Hall)
Rosewood (Warner Brothers, 1997, John Singleton)
Soul Food (Twentieth Century Fox, 1997, George Tillman Jr.)

1998

Belly (Artisan Entertainment, 1998, Hype Williams)
Down in the Delta (Miramax, 1998, Maya Angelou)
He Got Game (Touchstone, 1998, Spike Lee)
How Stella Got Her Groove Back (Twentieth Century Fox, 1998, Kevin Rodney Sullivan)
Ride (Miramax, 1998, Millicent Shelton)

1999

Funny Valentines (BET Pictures, 1999, Julie Dash)
Incognito (BET Pictures, 1999, Julie Dash)
Introducing Dorothy Dandridge (HBO, 1999, Martha Coolidge)

2000

Bamboozled (New Line Cinema, 2000, Spike Lee)
Disappearing Acts (HBO, 2000, Gina Prince-Blythewood)
Love and Basketball (New Line Cinema, 2000, Gina Prince-Blythewood)
Shaft (Paramount, 2000, John Singleton)

2001

Baby Boy (Columbia Pictures, 2001, John Singleton)
Bones (New Line Cinema, 2001, Ernest Dickerson)
Caveman's Valentine (Jersey Films, 2001, Kasi Lemmons)
Prison Song (New Line Cinema, 2001, Darnell Martin)
Stranger Inside (HBO, 2001, Cheryl Dunye)

BLACK FEMALE PROTAGONIST– DRIVEN NARRATIVES

Ghost (Paramount, 1990, Jerry Zucker)
The Long Walk Home (Miramax, 1990, Richard Pearce)
Strictly Business (Warner Brothers, 1991, Kevin Hooks)
Passion Fish (Miramax, 1992, John Sayles)
White Men Can't Jump (Twentieth Century Fox, 1992, Ron Shelton)
Zebrahead (Columbia Pictures, 1992, Anthony Drazan)
Sankofa (Mypheduh Films, 1993, Haile Gerima)
Just Another Girl on the I.R.T. (Miramax, 1993, Leslie Harris)
Made in America (Warner Brothers, 1993, Richard Benjamin)
Corrina, Corrina (New Line Cinema, 1994, Jesse Nelson)
The Incredibly True Story of Two Girls in Love (Fine Line, 1995, Maria Maggenti)
Losing Isaiah (Paramount, 1995, Stephen Gyllenhaal)
Strange Days (Twentieth Century Fox, 1995, Kathryn Bigelow)
Waiting to Exhale (Twentieth Century Fox, 1995, Forest Whitaker)
When Night Is Falling (October Films, 1995, Patricia Rozema)
The Associate (Buena Vista Pictures, 1996, Donald Petrie)
Girl 6 (Twentieth Century Fox, 1996, Spike Lee)
Set It Off (New Line Cinema, 1996, F. Gary Gray)
The Watermelon Woman (First Run Features, 1996, Cheryl Dunye)
Eve's Bayou (Trimark, 1997, Kasi Lemmons)
Jackie Brown (Miramax, 1997, Quentin Tarantino)
Bulworth (Twentieth Century Fox, 1998, Warren Beatty)
Down in the Delta (Miramax, 1998, Maya Angelou)
How Stella Got Her Groove Back (Twentieth Century Fox, 1998, Kevin Rodney Sullivan)
Introducing Dorothy Dandridge (HBO, 1999, Martha Coolidge)
Love and Basketball (New Line Cinema, 2000, Gina Prince-Blythewood)
Monster's Ball (Lions Gate Films, 2001, Marc Forster)
Swordfish (Warner Brothers, 2001, Dominic Sena)
Die Another Day (MGM, 2002, Lee Tamahori)
Gothika (Warner Brothers, 2003, Mathieu Kassovitz)

GENRE DIVISIONS

Black Family Films: Adults

To Sleep with Anger (Columbia Pictures, 1990, Charles Burnett)
Jungle Fever (Universal Pictures, 1991, Spike Lee)
I Like It Like That (Columbia Pictures, 1994, Darnell Martin)

Waiting to Exhale (Twentieth Century Fox, 1995, Forest Whitaker)
Soul Food (Twentieth Century Fox, 1997, George Tillman Jr.)
Down in the Delta (Miramax, 1998, Maya Angelou)
He Got Game (Touchstone, 1998, Spike Lee)
Caveman's Valentine (Jersey Films, 2001, Kasi Lemmons)

Black Family Films: Youth Focused

House Party (Columbia Pictures, 1990, Reginald Hudlin)
Boyz N the Hood (Columbia Pictures, 1991, John Singleton)
House Party II (Avco-Embassy, 1991, George Jackson and Doug McHenry)
Straight Out of Brooklyn (Samuel Goldwyn, 1991, Matty Rich)
Juice (Paramount, 1992, Ernest Dickerson)
Just Another Girl on the I.R.T. (Miramax, 1993, Leslie Harris)
Menace II Society (New Line Cinema, 1993, Allen and Albert Hughes)
Crooklyn (Universal Pictures, 1994, Spike Lee)
House Party III (New Line Cinema, 1994, Eric Meza)
Jason's Lyric (Polygram, 1994, Doug McHenry)
Sugar Hill a.k.a *Harlem* (Twentieth Century Fox, 1994, Leon Ichaso)
Clockers (Universal Pictures, 1995, Spike Lee)
Higher Learning (Columbia Pictures, 1995, John Singleton)
Eve's Bayou (Trimark, 1997, Kasi Lemmons)
Baby Boy (Columbia Pictures, 2001, John Singleton)

Black Romance

Strictly Business (Warner Brothers, 1991, Kevin Hooks)
Boomerang (Paramount, 1992, Reginald Hudlin)
Poetic Justice (Columbia Pictures, 1993, John Singleton)
How Stella Got Her Groove Back (Twentieth Century Fox, 1998, Kevin Rodney Sullivan)
Love and Basketball (New Line Cinema, 2000, Gina Prince-Blythewood)

Film Noir–Black Action Films

New Jack City (Warner Brothers, 1991, Mario Van Peebles)
One False Move (I.R.S. Media International, 1991, Carl Franklin)
Deep Cover (New Line Cinema, 1992, Bill Duke)
CB4 (Universal Pictures, 1993, Tamra Davis)
The Walking Dead (Savoy Pictures, 1995, Preston A. Whitmore II)
Dead Presidents (Buena Vista Pictures, 1995, Allen and Albert Hughes)
Devil in a Blue Dress (TriStar Pictures, 1995, Carl Franklin)

The Glass Shield (Miramax, 1995, Charles Burnett)
Original Gangstas (Orion Pictures, 1996, Larry Cohen; Fred Williamson, producer)
Gridlock'd (Polygram, 1997, Vondie Curtis-Hall)
Shaft (Paramount, 2000, John Singleton)

Social Satire: Politics, History, and Westerns

Posse (Polygram, 1993, Mario Van Peebles)
Panther (Polygram, 1995, Mario Van Peebles)
Get On the Bus (Columbia Pictures, 1997, Spike Lee)
Rosewood (Warner Brothers, 1997, John Singleton)
Bamboozled (New Line Cinema, 2000, Spike Lee)

Black Horror

Def by Temptation (Troma Films, 1990, James Bond III)
Tales from the Hood (Savoy Pictures, 1995, Rusty Cundieff)
Bones (New Line Cinema, 2001, Ernest Dickerson)

Index

African American film, 3, 4; defined, 1
African Diaspora, 1, 59n12, 116–117
American film industry, 14, 35, 50, 51,
    115
Apollo Theater, 8
Associate, The, 4, 5, 79, 86, 91, 92, 128,
    130; postNegritude womanist resis-
    tance in, 95–96; Whoopi Goldberg's
    whiteface gender-bending perform-
    ance, 95

Baker, Houston A., Jr., 95, 104n8
Bassett, Angela, 85, 97, 101
Bava, Mario, 75, 76
Berry, Halle, 4, 34, 90; acting career pre-
    Monster's Ball, 96–99, 101; Holly-
    wood casting and narrative limits for
    black women, 101–3
Birth of a Nation, The, 7
black action film, 4, 7, 13, 21, 37–59,
    131; Black Arts movement, black
    action film and its subgenre Black
    Gangster film, 52–56; defined, 4, 37;
    law and order in, 40–41; women-
    centered black action, 90, 109
black consciousness, as not racially
    exclusive, 4; its philosophical influ-
    ence on the aesthetics of black film,
    10, 51; *Sankofa*'s enlightened black
    consciousness for the 1990s, 112
black documentary filmmakers, 9
black family film, 14–36, 108; *Bush
    Mama* as black independent family/

action film, 108; class distinctions in,
    19–23; magical and social realism in,
    33; womanism and family film, 31
black horror film, 4, 68; as genre, 61–64
black independent filmmakers, 9–10,
    13; anti-imperialist struggles as
    influential to the style and politics of
    black independent filmmakers, 9;
    L.A. rebellion, 11
black-oriented film, 2, 3, 5, 9, 109;
    defined, 1
Black Power movement, 9, 51
black westerns, 57
blaxploitation, 7, 59n15, 121; usefulness
    of term to describe black action films,
    56–57
Bond, James, III, 64, 65, 127, 132
Bones, 4, 68–76, 77, 77nn7–8, 77n10,
    77n12, 122, 129, 132; 1970s nostal-
    gia in, 70; homoerotic sadomasoch-
    ism in, 70–71; audience for, 72;
    Snoop Dogg's aesthetic of cool, 72;
    women in, 70, 72–73
Bourne, St. Clair, 9, 10, 63, 108, 118n3,
    121
box-office receipts, 15, 16, 64, 101, 115,
    116
Burnett, Charles, 10, 11, 14, 16n8,
    17n12, 21, 33, 110, 115, 127, 128,
    130, 132; *Killer of Sheep*, 17, 19, 110

Civil Rights, as movement or era, 2, 9,
    36, 44, 51, 121
class, 3–4, 8, 11, 20, 21, 30, 33, 35, 36,
    39, 80–81, 88, 91; mobility, 21, 35,

133

About the Author

Mark A. Reid is professor of English and film at the University of Florida at Gainesville, where he teaches African Diasporic studies. He is the author of *Redefining Black Film* (1993) and *PostNegritude Visual and Literary Culture* (1997), the editor of *Spike Lee's "Do the Right Thing"* (1997), and the coeditor of *Le Cinéma noir américain* (1988). His work has also appeared as book chapters in *Cinemas of the Black Diaspora*, *Film Genre Reader II*, *Ex-Iles: Essays on Caribbean Cinema*, *The Passionate Camera*, *Paul Robeson: Artist and Citizen*, and *Trajectories: Inter-Asia Cultural Studies* and as articles in such journals as *American Literature*, *Black American Literature Forum*, *Black Film Review*, *Criticism*, *Film History*, *Film Quarterly*, *Jump Cut*, *Quarterly Review of Film and Video*, and *Research in African Literatures*. He has taught at the University of California-Davis, Indiana University-Bloomington, the University of Iowa, Notre Dame University, and the University of Ouagadougou in Burkina Faso (West Africa). In 1999, the University of Florida awarded him a Research Foundation Professorship.